—— THE ——
CHINA STUDY
FAMILY
COOKBOOK

THE
CHINA STUDY
FAMILY
COOKBOOK

100 RECIPES TO BRING YOUR FAMILY
TO THE PLANT-BASED TABLE

DEL SROUFE

EDITED BY LeANNE CAMPBELL, PhD

BenBella Books, Inc.
Dallas, TX

BenBella Books, Inc.
10440 N. Central Expressway, Suite 800
Dallas, TX 75231
www.benbellabooks.com
Send feedback to feedback@benbellabooks.com

Printed in the United States of America
10 9 8 7 6 5 4 3 2 1

Library of Congress Cataloging-in-Publication Data
Names: Sroufe, Del, author.
Title: The China study family cookbook : 100 recipes to bring your family to
    the plant-based table / Del Sroufe ; edited by LeAnne Campbell.
Description: Dallas, TX : BenBella Books, 2017. | Includes bibliographical
    references and index.
Identifiers: LCCN 2016047876 (print) | LCCN 2016048413 (ebook) | ISBN
    9781944648114 (paperback) | ISBN 9781944648121 (electronic)
Subjects: LCSH: Vegetarian cooking. | Cooking (Vegetables) | LCGFT: Cookbooks.
Classification: LCC TX837 .S7163 2017 (print) | LCC TX837 (ebook) | DDC
    641.6/5—dc23
LC record available at https://lccn.loc.gov/2016047876

Editing by LeAnne Campbell, Karen Wise, and Leah Wilson
Copyediting by Karen Levy
Proofreading by Laura Cherkas and Amy Zarkos
Indexing by Debra Bowman Indexing Services
Text design by Faceout Studio, Paul Nielson
Text composition by Aaron Edmiston
Front cover photo by Nicole Axeworthy
Front cover design by Faceout Studio, Emily Weigel
Full cover design by Sarah Avinger
Interior photography by Lindsay Dorka
Printed by Versa Press

Distributed by Perseus Distribution
www.perseusdistribution.com

To place orders through Perseus Distribution:
Tel: (800) 343-4499
Fax: (800) 351-5073
E-mail: orderentry@perseusbooks.com

Special discounts for bulk sales (minimum of 25 copies) are available. Please contact Aida Herrera at aida@benbellabooks.com.

CONTENTS

SALADS AND SALAD FIXINGS

SANDWICHES

SOUPS

ENTRÉES

CASEROLES

At Home with the Plant-Based Family
PAM FROST 237

DESSERTS

FOREWORD

As a parent, I know well that we want our kids to have the best of everything. I believe that we, as humans, are hardwired to want to increase the chances that our children will be successful. But how do we do that? Parenting is a tricky, difficult business.

Often we teach our kids by simply passing on the lessons and activities we've learned from our own life. We share the pastimes we enjoy and our values and attitudes regarding everything from politics to work to religion. Even though we may not be making a conscious effort to "teach" our kids during most times of the day, they are constantly watching and learning by observation.

When it comes to our health and the foods we eat, this dynamic can unfortunately lead to a dangerous situation. About 70 percent of Americans are overweight or obese, and diabetes is becoming more and more common. Heart disease, a disease strongly affected by diet, remains our number one killer. Among U.S. adults aged 55 to 64, about 75 percent take a prescription medication and roughly 20 percent are on five or more prescription medications every month. We are generally less healthy than we'd like to be, and we're medicated to the point where it has become normal to be taking daily medication.

Our diet is largely to blame, though physical inactivity is obviously an important contributor. Americans consume about 60 percent of their calories from "ultra-processed foods." Ultra-processed foods are a mishmash of multiple processed ingredients, including salt, refined sugars and fats, and various additives to boost color, flavor, or other qualities. These are foods like packaged cookies, snack items, and candies, to name a few examples. The human body does not perform optimally or sustain maximum health with this type of fuel, yet the majority of all our calories are ultra-processed!

I was at a wedding recently with my toddler, and the waitstaff, by default, assumed that our son would need a kid's menu. Of course the kid's menu consisted of choices like chicken fingers, pizza, and mac and cheese. To begin with, it's unfortunate that people assume kids need food that's different from what adults eat. Our expectations for our kids have become too low if we just assume they will never try new foods or foods that aren't hyperpalatable. In our push to get kids to eat all their food all the time, we have loaded their plates with extra fats and sugars and refined flours even beyond what the standard U.S. adult already consumes.

Our kids are learning our standard eating patterns all too well, and many are already paying the price. In the past thirty years, obesity has more than doubled among children and quadrupled among adolescents. Over 20 percent of adolescents are now obese. Diabetes is on the rise. Most studies show that our kids are eating way too many added sugars, processed foods, and animal foods, and not enough fruits, vegetables, or whole grains, as well as being far too sedentary. As a society, we are sending our kids down a path to poor health, illness, medication, and medical intervention, which will inevitably lead to personal tragedy—not to mention financial difficulty—for a great many people in the future.

I strongly believe that parents want the best for their kids, and that gives me hope. Unfortunately, though, many parents are uncertain of the best path. We are understandably worried about feeding kids new and different foods. Can they grow if they don't have meat? Are added oils and added sugars really that bad? And isn't dairy required for strong bones and teeth? You may have heard headlines about vegan kids who died or suffered permanent damage from a poorly planned diet. In the face of uncertainty surrounding something as precious as our children's health, we revert to the societal defaults because we don't want to take unnecessary risks. Many people have dabbled in plant-based diets for themselves, but once they have kids to feed, they put meat and dairy right back on the menu.

So let's work on changing the default nutritional choices, one person at a time. We can do better, and it starts in our home. It can start with this book. With some education, we all can view a meal of fruits, vegetables, whole grains, and legumes as healthy and normal, rather than radical.

Well-planned plant-based diets are marvelously healthy for kids and adults alike. In fact, a recent trial showed that parents and kids who adopt a strict plant-based diet together can lower their weight and reduce various risk factors for heart disease. Another study showed that cutting down dramatically on added sugar consumption has exceptional benefits in just two weeks. And while it is important to make sure that kids eat a varied plant-based diet with plenty of calories and get enough supplemental vitamin B_{12} and perhaps vitamin D in certain circumstances (see *The China Study Solution*), adding more fruits, vegetables, and whole grains to your family's meals will always be a good idea. Give your family more fiber and more antioxidants, and you'll give them more health.

The book you now hold is a wonderful book to bring kids and families back into the kitchen to enjoy food and health together. The recipes Chef Del shares and the techniques he teaches will serve you and your family well for years to come.

Just like we should tell our kids about the values of hard work, being kind and generous, and planning and saving for the future, it's equally if not more important to tell them how to protect and maintain good health. By simply starting with yourself and setting a good example, you will be a wonderful teacher and guide for your children and your family. In families with reluctant kids or spouses, making healthier choices for yourself will be an example that can be a powerful lesson, one that will bear fruit later in life, if not sooner. Though family dynamics do not ever feel simple or easy, making the right food choices can be surprisingly straightforward.

We love our children. They are our world. We love our parents. Our families are so instrumental to our lives, at all stages. Let's protect them and heal them, cherish and enjoy them. Start with food and health. I sincerely hope you enjoy this book, along with the other China Study cookbooks, and that they help you, at least in some small way, travel a path with greater health, happiness, and fulfillment. To you and your family's health!

–Thomas M. Campbell II, MD

INTRODUCTION

Nothing brings a family together like food—eating it and, at least in my family, cooking it.

I grew up surrounded by really good cooks. My father's mother and sisters were known around Brown County, Ohio, for their cooking. I remember as a child sitting in the kitchen and watching my grandmother cook—at least until she got tired of me hovering and sent me outside to play. I never saw her use a written recipe, and I never saw her measure any ingredient, even when she made a cake. She was one of *those* cooks, a master in the kitchen who had been cooking since she was a young girl.

My mother was the same way, but she was more experimental than my grandmother. She would occasionally try new dishes or take a recipe from the newspaper and reinvent it to her liking. Her pumpkin bread was so good she was asked to make it to sell at a small convenience store in downtown Columbus, Ohio, where we lived.

Both she and my grandmother cooked food that I would later come to know as American comfort food: fried chicken, meatloaf, roast turkey, baked ham, spaghetti and meatballs, grilled cheese sandwiches with tomato soup, hamburgers with French fries. They made everything from scratch.

Many years after my grandmother passed, I adopted first a vegan diet, and then a whole foods diet. My mother struggled for years with my dietary choices, not understanding that the way I choose to eat now is not an attack on the way I ate growing up. Nor did she understand at first that my food choices are not an attempt to rebel, but to save my own life. Many times I would go to visit her and she would want to cook for me. She would make one of my favorite dishes, fried chicken, thinking that I could take the day off from my diet and enjoy the food that I had always loved so much. It hurt her feelings that I would not eat her food. Over time she has come to understand more why I eat the way I do, as she has seen her own health improvements from cutting back on meat and dairy, and is now one of the biggest fans of my food, but especially at first, our relationship was strained.

Because what we eat and how we prepare it are such essential parts of family life, they can be hard things to change. Starting to eat healthier food as a family can be challenging, particularly in the beginning. Understanding the need to adopt a whole foods, plant-based diet as described in *The China Study* is one thing; knowing what that looks like on your dinner plate is something else. And figuring out how to cook for your family in a new, healthier way can feel like the most daunting challenge of all. Will your family like what you cook? What do you do if some of your family members decide they don't want to eat this way?

Older children (and even other grown-ups in your household) may be used to turning on the oven only for reheating convenience foods and frozen dinners. Getting them on board with the new eating plan may require a lot more effort, and you may not have absolute success, especially at first. After all, the older we become, the harder it is to change our habits.

The key to lasting change is the motivation to create the new habits that will carry you into the future. Your own motivation is easy—you've studied all the literature or seen a film like *Forks Over Knives* or *PlantPure Nation*. You wouldn't have bought this cookbook if you weren't motivated to eat differently. But your family may not be quite there with you yet. And that can make establishing new habits much harder.

The China Study Family Cookbook is here to help.

The recipes in this book, as in all the China Study cookbooks, are made solely from whole plant-based foods. They're oil-free and naturally low in fat, while high in flavor and nutrition. But the recipes in this book were created specifically with families in mind: They're classic American home-style dishes and other familiar foods that will help make the transition to healthier eating easier.

Many of the recipes I chose to include in this cookbook are dishes that I enjoyed as a kid. For instance, I loved rich, creamy macaroni and cheese growing up. It was a special treat at home and always included on my grandmother's holiday table. The first time I tried vegan mac and cheese, I was very disappointed. It was awful! It was nothing like the version I grew up with and left me feeling like I would never eat mac and cheese again. My recipe for Mac and Cheese (page 224), on the other hand, is familiar—creamy, with a mild, tangy flavor that even my most cheese-loving friends were impressed with. I use the sauce in that recipe to make everything from Sausage, Pepper, and Mushroom Pizza (page 208) to Grilled Cheese Sandwiches (page 145) to Quesadillas (page 187)—all dishes I remember loving as a kid.

Breakfast was a big deal in my family, especially on the weekends. My grandmother, who lived with my father when I was a teenager, would always make sausage, bacon, biscuits, and eggs for the first meal of the day, foods we rarely ate at home with Mom. We always had cereal and toast for breakfast during the week because Mom had to work and there was no time for cooking. Occasionally, though, Mom would make pancakes for dinner and, on rare occasions, sausage gravy and biscuits. My plant-based versions of these special breakfast foods have all the flavor of those original dishes without the heaviness that used to leave me in a fog for the rest of the day.

I love being able to have an occasional sweet treat without feeling as if I have ruined all my hard work to get healthier. One of my favorite desserts has always been the traditional Fudgsicle. It's a perfect, kid-friendly summer treat, creamy and cold and chocolaty. My version of Chocolate Pops (page 249), like all the dessert recipes in this cookbook, calls for no sugar, no animal products, and no added fats but is just as delicious as the ones I remember from my childhood.

The recipes in this book are made with familiar ingredients you won't have to go to specialty stores to find and with techniques that don't require a culinary degree to master. They include notes and tips for cooking with kids of all ages, or with anyone new to the plant-based way of cooking, or to the kitchen generally!

About the Interviews

People always ask me how I decided to adopt a low-fat, whole foods, plant-based diet. I've told my story many times at events I've attended and to anyone who's asked. Many have told me that my story inspired them to change their own eating habits, and some have shared their own stories with me. I tell my story, even when it has not been easy for me to do so, because it seems to help others. Change has sometimes been hard for me, and telling people about my struggles helps them understand that although this change can be difficult, it *can* be done.

The interviews in this book come from well-known leaders in the plant-based community, like T. Colin Campbell, author of *The China Study*, and Pam Popper, my business partner at Wellness Forum Health (where I work as executive chef and as an instructor for our Institute for Health Studies), along with families I know through my work there. They share how they got motivated to change their diet, the challenges they faced along the way, and their best advice for getting the whole family involved. Some found it easy to get the whole family on board with their new healthy eating plan. Others live in households where some do not eat this way, and you'll learn how they manage to cook for everyone with minimal stress. A few families, through patience and perseverance, have seen family members who at one time were resistant to change slowly come around and adopt this healthiest of eating plans.

I hope that reading these stories will inspire you to talk with your own family, change your diet, improve your health, and enjoy the journey with healthy, great-tasting food. And remember: Sharing your story with others can inspire them, too. By sharing, you can help grow a movement to change the health of our families, in America and around the world.

GETTING STARTED

EASING THE TRANSITION TO A PLANT-BASED DIET

Changing the way your family thinks about what they eat is not going to happen overnight. But here are some tips to help it go more smoothly, and especially to get your kids on board.

Stay with the Familiar

I can't stress this enough. If you start off with some strange-smelling stew with ingredients no one has ever heard of, your family is not going to buy in. Kids like routine, and they like to know what to expect. Once they get used to the family's new diet plan, then you can begin to introduce new flavors and textures. But for now, stick with what they know.

Most people prepare only a handful of dishes with any regularity. Look at those dishes you already prepare and find healthier substitutions for the unhealthy ingredients. If your family likes pizza—and what family doesn't?—then make a healthy pizza. Kids love French fries, so why not offer them an oil-free version? If you have a mac and cheese family, find a recipe that is similar to the one your family is used to (see page 224 for mine). Try a new taco recipe if your kids are fans of Tex-Mex cuisine. Use brown rice instead of white rice. Make a stir-fry without oil and see if they notice the difference.

And just because you're making a big change to your diet doesn't mean you have to suddenly become a gourmet chef. Learn to make simple meals a part of your menu planning. Soup and salad can be just as satisfying as a five-course meal, so save those gourmet dishes for special occasions.

Get the Kids Involved

If cooking with your kids is a new thing, there are plenty of tips in this book for getting them involved in meal preparation at home. Let them be a part of menu planning, shopping, putting away the groceries, prepping, cooking, cleaning up afterward, and, of course, eating the delicious food they helped prepare.

Just because you're the grown-up doesn't mean you have to do everything! With a little guidance (and patience) from you, kids can help at every stage. But don't overwhelm them—younger kids may not have the interest or ability to prepare a dish from beginning to end. Let them work on one task at a time, making sure that it is age-appropriate and that it interests them.

Letting kids help with menu planning will give them a vested interest in seeing the plan through to the dinner table. Talk to your children about cooking in season and let them help pick out dishes; when they get older, you can teach them about the food budget.

Be Patient!

The transition to a plant-based diet is not as simple as flipping a switch. At first you may even need to persuade other grown-ups in your household, as well as the kids, to go along with the plan. Don't give up if you meet with initial resistance. Some people have more trouble with change than others, so let them take their time.

Once you get cooking, remember that kids (and some grown-ups!) may have short attention spans and don't always have an easy time following instructions. Don't be in a rush to have your kids cooking an entire meal the first time out. Give them a specific task and show them how you want it done. If they complete that task and are still with you, give them another task. Your patience will pay off down the road with kids who are not only capable cooks in the kitchen but also more likely to become adventurous eaters willing to try new foods.

COOKING AT EVERY AGE

There are two important factors to consider when deciding which tasks your child is able to perform in the kitchen: their physical ability to do the task and their mental ability to comprehend the task and, in particular, the possible dangers involved.

Young children will not have the strength to lift pots and pans or to cut through dense foods like potatoes, but they also may not know that hot foods can burn them or that knives are dangerous. Younger kids also may have trouble remembering a series of steps that need to be followed, so you can help them by breaking down a task step by step as they go along. They definitely need to show that they can follow directions before you let them handle dangerous equipment.

You know your child better than anyone, but here are some tips for helping them get acquainted with the kitchen so that they can become proficient. It is important that your kids master each level before going on to more technical cooking activities.

The Youngest Cooks

Your eighteen-month-old probably wants to be a part of whatever you are doing in the kitchen—until they find the next thing to do. Children at this age obviously need the most supervision, since their motor skills are not yet highly developed and they have short attention spans.

Your child is never too young to learn the importance of cleanliness. Make this ongoing task a part of the cooking experience now and you will have cleanliness in the kitchen in the future. Hand washing and avoiding cross-contamination are important for even the youngest cooks to learn about. (Granted, cross-contamination is not as big a problem in the plant-based kitchen as it is in kitchens with meat or other animal products, but it is a good habit just the same.)

Children as young as eighteen months can do the simplest of tasks. They need supervision and may show interest for only a few minutes at a time, but let them do what they will even if it does not contribute in any but the smallest way to the task at hand. My friend's daughter used to come to my bakery regularly with her parents. Even before she was able to walk, I would give her a piece of bread dough to play with. Every time she came into my bakery she would want something to play with. As she got older, she would help her mom in the kitchen, setting the table, removing dirty dishes from the table, stirring cake batter, or adding a premeasured ingredient to a bowl. When she was a teenager, I hired her to help me with catering events, and to this day, she still helps her mom in the kitchen when she comes home from school.

3- to 5-Year-Old Cooks

Kids at this age are able to understand directions better and can help with more specific tasks such as measuring ingredients, chopping herbs with a butter knife, mashing potatoes, whisking salad dressing, or putting salad greens into a serving bowl.

Show children the difference between wet and dry measuring cups, how to level dry ingredients using the straight edge of a butter knife, and how to measure liquid ingredients to the line indicating the quantity called for in the recipe.

Kids at this age are too young for even basic math, but they can certainly count out items with you.

5- to 7-Year-Old Cooks

School-age children can engage in more technical activities and use more sophisticated equipment. They can handle measuring, mixing, pouring, grating, and peeling, as well as setting the table. They still need constant supervision, but you may let them use a sharp knife—keeping in mind that the size of the knife should be appropriate for the child's hand and ability to manage it.

Adults should advise younger children that hot foods can cause serious burns, especially because young kids may have even more sensitive skin and mouths than adults.

8- to 11-Year-Old Cooks

Kids at this age can follow simple, straightforward recipes, plan menus and meals, and begin to work with the stove or oven. Use this time to teach them about the dangers of equipment and utensils. Talk to them about taking their time, doing one activity at a time, and using gloves to handle hot items (you may need to buy them their own in a size that fits their smaller hands).

This age group can probably handle a can opener. Show them how to do it on a stable surface. They can also learn about cooking times, cooking temperatures, and testing for doneness in baked goods. They can practice their math skills to double or halve ingredient quantities (see page 33).

12-Year-Old and Up Cooks

Older children can start to improvise and prepare more complex recipes, often unsupervised. Kids who exhibit good kitchen safety skills, as described in the next section, can even use equipment like blenders and food processors.

WHY TEACH KIDS TO COOK

After my parents got divorced, my dad had to learn how to cook for himself, and he patiently allowed me into the kitchen with him as he figured it out. The first recipes I remember cooking with him were found on the back of the Bisquick box: pancakes and streusel coffee cake. I wasn't the most helpful sous chef to my dad, at least not in the beginning, but we both learned as we went along.

It was some years later before I cooked dinner for my working mother. I was intimidated because she was so good in the kitchen, but I felt bad for her, coming home from work every day and having to prepare dinner for her three kids. One day, I got over my nervousness and cooked a dinner of roasted chicken with herbed green beans for the whole family. She was surprised and delighted when she came home from work. Her pride and joy upon learning that I could cook, and the patience my father showed me in his kitchen, encouraged me to cook more for my family, and eventually for friends, and now for the general public. Not every meal I cooked along the way was a winner, but the practice, support, and praise I received gave me the confidence to continue cooking and eventually to do it for a living.

I can't say enough about the importance of getting children interested in cooking at a young age, since kids who cook become adults who cook. While younger kids may sometimes be more of a hindrance than a help in the kitchen, with patience and practice, those messy young sous chefs will one day cook entire meals for the family—and even clean up the kitchen afterward! It's an investment well worth the spills and burned dishes early on.

Teaching your kids to cook helps them develop highly transferable skills, from how to do basic math (used for measuring ingredients) to how to see a project through from beginning to end. It teaches them patience, because cooking has its own timeline and can't be rushed—trying to do so usually ends in a less-than-desirable (and sometimes less-than-edible) result. Teaching kids to cook even teaches them the value of money, since cooking at home is far less expensive than eating out. Buying processed foods at the supermarket is more expensive than buying food you prepare at home, too—and usually not as healthy.

But most importantly, cooking with your kids is a great opportunity to talk about health and the difference between the standard American diet and a whole foods, plant-based diet. You can talk about the difference between healthy and unhealthy ingredients and between healthy and unhealthy cooking techniques. You can have conversations about why you don't use oil or why you use whole wheat flour instead of white flour. When you take them shopping with you for ingredients, you can show them how to read product labels, so they know the difference between real food and junk food.

Kids who cook become adults who cook and eat healthier than those who don't. Cooking plant-based meals with your kids not only brings your family together, but it can also give them the gift of a lifetime of health and well-being.

KITCHEN SAFETY

Danger is everywhere in the kitchen, so before you let your children in there with you, make sure your cooking space is as safe as possible for everyone. Spend time with your children talking about the following kitchen safety rules to help keep them free from danger.

Cleanliness

Kitchen cleanliness is an important part of kitchen safety. A dirty kitchen can cause illness and even injury. Always wash your hands before starting to cook. Use warm, soapy water and scrub your hands for 20 seconds, then dry them thoroughly. Clean hands are safe hands for handling pots, pans, knives, and other equipment—as well as food!

Clean up spills as soon as they happen. Wet floors are dangerous. So are obstacles: keep the kitchen floor clear of toys, shoes, and other items.

Put tools away as soon as you finish using them.

Stoves, Ovens, and Microwaves

Children should not be allowed to use the stove or oven until they are tall enough to reach all its components with ease, strong enough to lift and carry pots and pans with hot food in them, and capable of understanding the inherent dangers.

If your child is using a gas stove for the first time, be sure to show them the difference between a low, medium, and high flame.

Never leave the kitchen with pots and pans cooking on the stove. Turn off burners as soon as you take the pot off. Remind children that even after a stove or an oven is turned off, it stays hot for quite a while and can still cause burns.

Make sure handles of pots and pans are turned away from the front of the stove. Burns from scalding are far more common than thermal burns—that is, young children are more likely to burn themselves by reaching up for a pot or pan handle and then spilling hot liquid on themselves than by grabbing a hot object.

Teach kids to carefully open a pot lid away from them, as steam can come out under pressure and scald them.

Never leave oven mitts or kitchen towels near the stove. Even after a stove burner is turned off (especially electric), cloth can catch fire. For the same reason, avoid wearing loose-fitting clothes (especially long, flowing sleeves) while cooking, and pull back long hair into a ponytail.

Never place metal objects in the microwave. Teach your kids that even though the microwave itself does not get hot, the foods or liquids that come out of it can be very hot and cause serious injury.

Keep a fire extinguisher in or near the kitchen, but not near the stove or the heater.

Knives

Keep knives sharpened. Sharp knives are actually safer to use than dull knives, because food is easier to cut with less force, so you have greater control over the cutting object.

Teach your kids to hold a knife by the handle in a fashion similar to shaking someone's hand. Never touch the blade of a knife.

Practice the claw-and-saw method of cutting, and show your kids: While holding the knife in one hand, curl the fingers of the hand holding the food being chopped into a "claw" to protect the fingers from the sharp blade. If the knife blade gets too close to the other hand, it will only touch the fingernails, not the fingertips.

Carry knives with the cutting edge slightly away from your body. Rather than handing a knife to another person, set it down on the counter or table and let the other person pick it up.

Never leave knives in a sink or pan full of soapy water. They should be washed, dried, and put away immediately after use to avoid the risk of injury.

Using Equipment and Tools Properly

Never use equipment for tasks other than those it was intended for. You run the risk of damaging the equipment—and also causing injury.

Pots and Pans

If you are using nonstick pans, use only rubber/silicone or wooden spatulas to cook with. Metal utensils can scrape off the finish and render them useless and potentially toxic.

Blenders and Food Processors

Use these two tools as they are designed to be used and they can last many years. Blenders are meant to puree liquids, while food processors are meant to chop solid foods. (There are some in-between ingredients and recipes that can go either way, like silken tofu.) Use each appliance only as directed by the manufacturer.

Unplug the blender and food processor when cleaning and when not in use. Keep the power cord away from stove burners.

Always use the food pusher to feed food into the chute of the food processor. Never use your fingers, knives, spatulas, or other implements to push food into the chute.

Never put your fingers, knives, spatulas, or other tools into the bowl of a food processor or blender while the motor is running.

Remove the lid only after the motor has come to a complete stop.

Never immerse the base of the blender or food processor in water to wash it.

Knives

Knives come in different shapes and sizes. Younger hands may be most comfortable with a paring knife, but for older kids, choose the right knife for the job. A paring knife is ideal for peeling, a chef's knife is great for chopping, and a serrated knife is perfect for slicing bread or pastries.

Do not use your best chef's knife as a can opener. It is a fragile instrument and can easily break.

Always wash your knives with warm soapy water—never in the dishwasher. The hot water will dull the blades.

Have your knives professionally sharpened once a year, but hone them regularly at home. Buy a good honing tool and learn how to use it. Many cooking stores have associates trained to teach you this skill. Maintain your knives and they will last you many years.

TIPS FOR NEW COOKS

Menu Planning and Shopping

It should come as no surprise that when you involve your kids in menu planning as well as meal preparation and cooking, they will be more eager to try new foods. Depending on their age, kids might plan an entire meal (within reason!), with you helping them figure out which dishes will go well together and make for a balanced meal.

Whenever possible, take the kids with you to the grocery store. Show them how to read ingredient labels, compare prices, and select fresh, ripe produce.

Teach your kids that most processed foods cost more than cooking them yourself. For example, compare the prices of bags of dried beans and cans of cooked beans. Point out that the beans you cook from dried are about one-quarter the price of the canned variety. Explain that cooking beans from scratch takes more time than opening a can, and on a very busy day you may want to spend a little extra money for that convenience. These conversations will help your kids begin to understand how purchasing decisions can affect the food budget.

This same lesson can be applied to fresh, in-season produce compared to canned or frozen, red bell peppers that you roast yourself versus the kind that come already roasted in a jar, and so on.

Preparing to Cook

Preparing your space and ingredients is one of the most important parts of the cooking process. Whenever you start a recipe, do the following things to make your cooking go smoothly and safely:

1. Read through the recipe so you know which tools and ingredients you will need and you can be ready for each step. This is also a good time to review the recipe to see how much supervision you will need to provide. Most recipes require adult supervision for younger cooks, and you should use this time to teach the young ones about kitchen safety and the tools used in each recipe. Determine which tasks can be assigned to which kids. (See page 23 for more on cooking at different ages.)

2. Make sure your kitchen prep areas are clean and uncluttered.

3. Gather your ingredients and tools. This is known as *mise en place*, which means to "put in place." Your cooking experience will go much more smoothly if you take the time to set everything up beforehand. You will also avoid unplanned trips to the store when you realize you are out of some ingredients. Note also that some recipes call for other subrecipes to be completed ahead of time. For instance, my Breakfast Sandwiches (page 68) come together in a flash— but only if you've already prepared the Biscuits (page 50); Asparagus, Leek, and Mushroom Frittata (page 66); Spicy Breakfast Patties (page 56); and Mayonnaise (page 97). Planning ahead pays off!

4. Wash your hands before you start prepping and cooking.

Measuring Ingredients

Liquids and dry ingredients require two different kinds of measurements and two different kinds of measuring cups. Liquid measurements are best done in a clear glass or plastic measuring cup so you can place the cup on a flat surface and pour the liquid up to the desired measurement line. It helps to squat or bend down so that the cup is at eye level.

To measure a dry ingredient like flour, use a measuring cup with a specific measurement. If you need 1 cup of flour, scoop a 1-cup measure into the flour, then use the flat side of a knife or spatula to scrape off the excess above the rim of the cup.

Kitchen Math Basics

A well-written recipe will make math practically unnecessary when preparing a dish, but what happens when you want to double or halve a recipe? Measurement conversions are an important part of cooking, so a measurement conversion chart like the one below is a necessity if you are not used to doing these calculations in your head. You can also find conversion charts online.

To help kids practice their math, give them exercises with recipes that require them to convert measurements from, say, tablespoons to cups. For example,

1 cup = 16 tablespoons, but it is easier to measure 1 cup than to measure out 16 individual tablespoons

Triple 3 tablespoons in a recipe and you get 9 tablespoons, or ½ cup + 1 tablespoon

Measurement Conversions

1 tablespoon = 3 teaspoons

⅟₁₆ cup = 1 tablespoon

⅛ cup = 2 tablespoons

⅙ cup = 2 tablespoons + 2 teaspoons

¼ cup = 4 tablespoons

⅓ cup = 5 tablespoons + 1 teaspoon

⅜ cup = 6 tablespoons

½ cup = 8 tablespoons

⅔ cup = 10 tablespoons + 2 teaspoons

¾ cup = 12 tablespoons

1 cup = 16 tablespoons

8 fluid ounces = 1 cup

1 pint = 2 cups

1 quart = 2 pints

4 cups = 1 quart

1 gallon = 4 quarts

16 ounces = 1 pound

Oil-Free Cooking

Preparing oil-free dishes can take some getting used to, since some ingredients fare better in an oil-free pan than others.

For sautéing, water-soluble vegetables are easily adapted to the oil-free pan. Steam is released from these foods, which buffers them against the heat. These foods can be cooked in a dry skillet, allowing them to caramelize to achieve richer flavor. The following water-soluble vegetables are easily sautéed in a dry pan or with just a small amount of added water:

Asparagus
Bell peppers
Cabbage
Carrots
Celery
Greens like spinach, kale, and chard
Mung bean sprouts
Mushrooms
Onions
Tomatoes
Zucchini

Cauliflower and broccoli have a high water content, but they don't release their water as readily as other vegetables, so you'll get better results by boiling them in water or roasting them in the oven. Potatoes release starch and water together, so they tend to stick to the pan—again, boiling or roasting is the way to go here.

Oil- and Sugar-Free Baking

Baking without fat or sugar poses a few challenges even for experienced bakers. Both fat and sugar help make the finished product tender. To compensate for the loss of these tenderizers, I have reduced the amount of flour in my recipes and, in some cases, added applesauce, which has a pectin in it that acts as a tenderizer.

The baked goods in this cookbook call for pastry flour, which is made from soft wheat berries and yields a tender crumb in baked goods. Look for whole wheat pastry flour, if possible, but not plain whole wheat flour (often labeled whole wheat bread flour), which is better suited for making bread.

Many of my recipes for sweet treats call for pureed white beans. That may seem strange, but you can think of it as using unprocessed tofu, which is also made from beans and is widely used in nondairy dessert recipes. When presenting children with new or unusual dishes like these, don't dramatize it. They respond to the world as you do. Instead, treat unusual-sounding recipes like any other recipe you would make.

Regarding sweet treats, remember that they are still just that—treats—and should not be eaten with abandon just because they are free of processed sugars and fat. Flour, date puree, and peanut butter all contain concentrated calories that can easily contribute to weight gain if overeaten.

Different types of baked goods have different textures in part because of the way they are mixed. Bread doughs should be mixed more vigorously and for a longer period of time than other types of dough to activate the gluten in them. When making cookies, brownies, and other pastries, it's best to mix the dough gently and only long enough to incorporate the wet and dry ingredients together. In fact, we actually just "fold" the ingredients together by scooping the spatula under the dough and gently bringing it up and over the dough. This distinction is important with low-fat baking because fat usually protects the dough in pastries from overmixing.

If you set five ovens to 350°F and put an oven thermometer into each, they will all read a different temperature. Move the thermometer to different parts of each oven and again the temperatures will be different, since all ovens have their own "hot spots." Most ovens are off by about 25 degrees, so always keep an oven thermometer in yours and set your oven temperature according to the thermometer.

When the baking time called for in a recipe is a range, such as 25 to 30 minutes, check for doneness just before the early end of the recommended baking time. If it is not done, put it back in the oven and check it again every few minutes until it is done.

I use two methods for checking a baked good for doneness. The first is to insert a toothpick into the center of the baked item and pull it out. If some of the wet batter comes out with it, the item is not cooked through and should go back into the oven. Check it again in 5 minutes.

The second method is to touch the center of the baked good with your finger. If the item springs back after being touched, it is finished. If your finger leaves a dent in the item, it needs to cook longer.

NUTRITIONAL VALUE

To be consistent with the message in *The China Study* and especially its sequel, *Whole*, recipes in the China Study cookbook line do not include breakdowns of nutrient composition. Nutrient measurements in different samples of the same food are often highly variable, and it is far more important to focus on food variety and wholesomeness.

Instead, the following symbols are used to indicate which parts of the plant (or, in one case, plant type) each recipe incorporates:

GRAINS
Grains abound in carbohydrates, fiber, minerals, and B vitamins.

LEGUMES
Legumes are a hearty source of protein, fiber, and iron.

ROOTS
Roots are full of carbohydrates; some have carotenoids.

LEAVES
Leaves are lush with antioxidants, fiber, and complex carbohydrates.

FLOWERS
Flowers are rich in antioxidants and phytochemicals.

NUTS
Nuts are loaded with omega-3 fats, vitamin E, and protein.

MUSHROOMS
Mushrooms offer a significant supply of selenium and other antioxidants.

FRUITS
Fruits are packed with vitamin C and other phytochemicals.

It's important to consume a variety of categories each day in order to obtain all the nutrients you need for good health!

BREAKFAST

HOT COCOA

Long before instant cocoa was available, my mom would make us hot cocoa from scratch. I still love a good cup of cocoa, especially now that I can enjoy it without dairy and sugar. If your kids think that cocoa can only be prepared from a mix, it's time to show them how to make the real thing.

Serves 2

1½ cups unsweetened plant milk

½ cup Date Puree (page 241), or more to taste

¼ cup unsweetened cocoa

½ teaspoon pure vanilla extract

Pinch sea salt

1. Combine all the ingredients in a blender and process until smooth.
2. Pour the liquid into a small saucepan and cook over medium heat until steamy, about 5 minutes. Do not boil.
3. Pour into mugs and serve.

OATMEAL AND ALL THE FIXIN'S

Oatmeal with a choice of toppings is one of the easiest breakfast foods to have on hand for your family. Growing up, my brother liked his with raisins and brown sugar, but I liked cinnamon, sugar, and milk. Even today I eat it that way, only with plant milk instead of dairy and stevia in place of the sugar.

Serves 4

3¾ cups water

2 cups regular rolled oats

¼ teaspoon sea salt

Optional additions:

1 teaspoon ground cinnamon or pumpkin pie spice

Chopped dried fruits: dates, apples, apricots, raisins, currants, figs

Chopped fresh fruit: apples, pears, peaches, nectarines, plums, bananas, figs

Berries: strawberries, blueberries, blackberries, raspberries

Nuts (toasted or raw): walnuts, pecans, almonds, hazelnuts, pistachios

Seeds (toasted or raw): sunflower, sesame, chia, hemp, pumpkin, pomegranate

Unsweetened plant milk: soy, almond, oat, rice

1. Pour the water into a small saucepan with a tight-fitting lid. Bring it to a boil over medium heat.
2. Stir in the oats and sea salt and bring the water back to a boil. Reduce the heat to medium-low, cover the pan, and cook for 5 minutes, stirring occasionally.
3. Divide the oatmeal among four bowls and add optional toppings and mix-ins as desired.

📝 NOTE FOR THE COOK

Be extra cautious to avoid spattering hot oatmeal. Thick, creamy foods like oatmeal and creamed soups pose an added risk for burning as they tend to stick to the skin more readily than thin liquids and thus make burns worse.

CARROT CAKE BAKED OATMEAL

Serve this dish to the kids and tell them it's "dessert for breakfast." You won't have any problem getting them to sit down and eat.

Serves 6 to 8

2 cups regular rolled oats

½ cup chopped toasted pecans (see Note; optional)

2 teaspoons double-acting baking powder

1½ teaspoons ground cinnamon

½ teaspoon ground allspice

¼ teaspoon sea salt

2½ cups unsweetened plant milk

1½ cups grated carrots
1 cup Date Puree (page 241)
2 teaspoons pure vanilla extract

---

1. Preheat the oven to 350°F.
2. In a large bowl, combine the rolled oats, toasted pecans (if using), baking powder, cinnamon, allspice, and sea salt. Mix well and set the mixture aside.
3. In a medium-size bowl, whisk together the plant milk, carrots, date puree, and vanilla. Add the wet mixture to the dry mixture and stir until combined. Let the mixture sit for 20 minutes.
4. Pour the batter into a nonstick 9×13-inch baking dish. Bake until lightly browned on top, 35 to 40 minutes.
5. Let cool for about 10 minutes, then slice and serve.

📝 NOTE FOR THE COOK

You can toast nuts in the oven or on the stovetop. I prefer the oven method because it is a little more forgiving if I happen to walk away from the kitchen and leave them unattended. On the stovetop, nuts quickly go from toasted to burned, so you have to stay with them to avoid burning.

- Oven method: Preheat the oven to 350°F. Coarsely chop the nuts and spread them out on a rimmed baking sheet. Bake the nuts until fragrant and lightly browned, 7 to 8 minutes.

- Stovetop method: Coarsely chop the nuts and toast them in a skillet over medium-low heat, shaking the pan frequently, until fragrant and lightly browned, 4 to 5 minutes.

PANCAKES

I first made pancakes (using the recipe on the back of the Bisquick box) at age seven or eight. By the fourth or fifth time I made that recipe, I had learned how to cook them to the proper doneness. This recipe is almost as easy as the one on the box and is perfect for those hot-breakfast-in-a-hurry mornings.

Makes 12 pancakes

1½ cups whole wheat pastry flour

2 teaspoons double-acting baking powder

¼ teaspoon sea salt

¼ teaspoon ground nutmeg

1 cup unsweetened applesauce

1¼ cups unsweetened plant milk

½ teaspoon pure vanilla extract (optional)

Vanilla-Almond Dessert Sauce (page 242), for serving

Fresh fruit (such as berries or sliced bananas), for serving

1. In a medium-size bowl, whisk together the flour, baking powder, sea salt, and nutmeg.
2. Make a well in the center of the dry ingredients and add the applesauce, plant milk, and vanilla (if using). Using a wooden spoon or rubber spatula, gently fold the wet ingredients into the dry ingredients. Let the batter stand for 10 minutes.
3. Preheat a nonstick skillet over medium heat. Preheat the oven to 250°F.
4. Scoop ¼ cup of the batter into the skillet for each pancake, fitting as many as you can without allowing them to touch. Let the pancakes cook until the edges start to brown, 4 to 5 minutes. Turn the pancakes over and cook until the center of each pancake is firm to the touch, another 4 minutes or so.
5. Transfer the pancakes to a baking sheet and keep them warm in the oven while you prepare the remaining pancakes.
6. Serve the pancakes topped with the vanilla sauce and fresh fruit.

🍽 RECIPE TIP

Keep a variety of fresh or frozen fruits, chocolate chips, nuts, and seeds on hand so everyone can decide what they want in their pancakes. It doesn't take much more effort, and kids love designing their own pancakes. When they can show competence around the stove, they can make their own pancakes from start to finish.

To add these extra ingredients to the pancake batter, spoon the batter into the pan as usual and then scatter a few tablespoons of the desired topping(s) over each pancake. Take care when flipping the pancakes so that you don't dislodge the toppings. Of course, if everyone wants the same thing, you can mix the chosen topping directly into the batter.

Here are some popular topping suggestions:

Fresh or frozen raspberries, blueberries, or blackberries
Sliced bananas
Sliced apples and a sprinkle of ground cinnamon
Sliced pears
Sliced peaches, nectarines, or plums
Pineapple chunks with toasted chopped macadamia nuts and toasted unsweetened coconut flakes
Vegan chocolate chips
Chopped nuts
Toasted coconut flakes
Your favorite granola or muesli
Rolled oats
Toasted millet

📝 NOTE FOR THE COOK

The key to light, fluffy, oil-free pancakes is a good whole wheat pastry flour, not regular whole wheat flour. It's also important to avoid overmixing the batter, and then to let it sit for several minutes to rest. Finally, do not flip the pancakes until they are ready.

CHOCOLATE DOUGHNUTS

My mom never let us have foods like doughnuts for breakfast at home. She tried to make sure we had a healthy breakfast, and doughnuts had a reputation as the bad boy of breakfast foods. Rightfully so—until now. These doughnuts are not only whole grain but also free of oil and processed sugar, so you can include them on the list of healthy breakfast foods you serve to your family.

Makes 8 or 9 doughnuts

¾ cup whole wheat pastry flour

¼ cup unsweetened cocoa powder

1 teaspoon double-acting baking powder

¼ teaspoon sea salt

¾ cup unsweetened applesauce

¾ cup Date Puree (page 241)

¼ cup unsweetened plant milk

½ teaspoon pure vanilla extract

CHOCOLATE FROSTING

½ cup sweet potato puree (see Tip)

¼ cup Date Puree (page 241)

2 tablespoons almond butter

3 tablespoons unsweetened cocoa powder

1. Preheat the oven to 350°F.
2. In a medium-size bowl, whisk together the flour, cocoa powder, baking powder, and sea salt.
3. In a separate bowl, whisk together the applesauce, date puree, plant milk, and vanilla. Add the wet ingredients to the dry ingredients and stir until just combined.
4. Spoon or pipe the batter into eight or nine wells in a nonstick doughnut pan. Bake until the doughnuts spring back when gently pressed, 12 to 15 minutes.

Let the doughnuts cool slightly in the pan before transferring to a cooling rack to cool completely.

5. While the doughnuts are cooling, combine all the chocolate frosting ingredients in a food processor and puree until smooth and creamy.

6. Spread 2 to 3 tablespoons of the chocolate frosting over each doughnut. Serve.

🍽 RECIPE TIP

You can buy canned or frozen sweet potato puree at your grocery store, but you can also make your own version that is cheaper and better. Here's how:

1. Preheat the oven to 350°F.

2. Put 2 large sweet potatoes on a baking sheet and pierce each potato a few times with a fork. Bake until the potatoes are very tender, about 1 hour. Let the potatoes cool to room temperature.

3. Cut the potatoes in half and scoop the potato flesh from the skins into a food processor. Puree until smooth and creamy.

4. Store in an airtight container in the refrigerator for up to a week.

📝 NOTE FOR THE COOK

It is important not to overmix any batter or dough when baking, and especially when baking without oil or added fat. Overmixing causes the finished product to be tough and chewy.

📝 NOTE FOR THE COOK

Oil-free baked goods go from done to overdone very quickly. Watch the timer and check them in the last few minutes of baking. If they feel firm on top, they are done.

BISCUITS

My first attempt at biscuits (like my first pancakes, also from the recipe on the Bisquick box!) came out chewy because, as my Uncle Stanley frequently reminded me, I overmixed the batter. The key to tender biscuits made without the fat of traditional biscuits is in the flour and the mixing. Spelt flour, though high in protein (gluten), is a soft flour that gives a tender crumb in baked goods. The traditional dough has been replaced by a thick batter; to help give it shape, we bake the biscuits in a muffin tin.

Makes 8 or 9 biscuits

1¾ cups whole-grain spelt flour

1 tablespoon double-acting baking powder

½ teaspoon sea salt

1 cup unsweetened applesauce

½ cup unsweetened plant milk

3 tablespoons pure maple syrup (optional)

1. Preheat the oven to 425°F.
2. Whisk together the spelt flour, baking powder, and sea salt in a medium-size bowl. Make a well in the center of the flour mixture and add the applesauce, plant milk, and maple syrup (if using). Gently fold the liquid ingredients into the flour mixture. Do not overmix.
3. To form the biscuits, use a medium ice cream scoop or a ⅓-cup measure to fill eight or nine cups of a nonstick muffin tin two-thirds full.
4. Reduce the oven temperature to 375°F and bake until the biscuits are browned and firm to the touch, 12 to 13 minutes.

📝 NOTE FOR THE COOK

Oil-free baked goods go from done to overdone very quickly. Watch the timer and check them in the last few minutes of baking. If they feel firm on top, they are done.

BREAKFAST SPREAD

I'm generally against "healthy by deception" practices for kids (and finicky eaters of any age), but this recipe is so delicious that no one will suspect it's also good for them. This breakfast spread is free of processed sugar and made with high-fiber, vitamin-packed beans and bananas (the riper, the better). I spread it on toast when I need a quick breakfast on the go. It also makes a great filling for Whoopie Pies (page 262). The key to a creamy spread is not to rush the pureeing in the food processor.

Serves 8

1 cup cooked or canned white beans (see Tip)

2 ripe bananas

½ cup nut butter of choice

1 cup pitted dates

2 tablespoons unsweetened cocoa powder

1 tablespoon pure vanilla extract

Pinch sea salt (optional)

1. Combine all the ingredients in a food processor and puree until smooth and creamy.
2. Store in an airtight container in the refrigerator for up to a week.

 RECIPE TIP

Any white beans will work in this recipe—Great Northern, cannellini, or navy—so use whatever you have on hand.

 NOTE FOR THE COOK

Pitted dates sometimes still have pits in them, so always check each date before you put it in the food processor. If you do accidentally put one in the machine, you'll hear a ticking noise, letting you know it's there.

BREAKFAST POTATOES

You could really call these "anytime" potatoes, because they are easy to prepare and healthy enough to have as a late-night snack. This is a great recipe for the young cook to practice measuring, since it has only five ingredients.

Serves 6

4 pounds russet potatoes, peeled and diced

2 tablespoons arrowroot powder or cornstarch

1 tablespoon granulated onion

1 tablespoon granulated garlic

Sea salt and black pepper

1. Preheat the oven to 375°F.
2. Put the potatoes in a medium saucepan with enough water to cover them. Bring the water to a boil over high heat, reduce the heat to medium, and cook the potatoes until they start to soften, about 5 minutes. Do not fully cook them, as they will finish cooking in the oven.
3. Drain the water from the potatoes and add the arrowroot powder, granulated onion, granulated garlic, and sea salt and black pepper to taste. Toss well to combine.
4. Spread the potatoes in a single layer on a nonstick baking sheet. Bake the potatoes until they start to brown and crisp, about 30 minutes. Serve warm.

📝 NOTE FOR THE COOK

The key to cutting potatoes safely is carefully cutting them in half so that they sit with stability on the work surface, and then cutting each half as you wish.

📝 NOTE FOR THE COOK

Roasting potatoes or other root vegetables without oil requires good timing. Undercook them and they don't taste like much; overcook them and they get tough and chewy. Paying close attention to the potatoes in the last few minutes of baking is crucial.

SPICY BREAKFAST PATTIES

When I was growing up, we usually had oatmeal and whole-grain toast with butter and jam for breakfast during the week. Foods like sausage, biscuits, and eggs were considered weekend fare. These patties are a great alternative to the traditional versions made from pork.

Makes 14 to 16 patties

2 cups water

1 cup millet

¼ cup minced yellow onion

4 garlic cloves, minced

2 sun-dried tomatoes, minced

2 tablespoons tamari, or to taste

½ teaspoon dried sage

1 teaspoon crushed fennel seeds

1 teaspoon crushed red pepper flakes, or to taste

¼ cup nutritional yeast

Sea salt

---

1. Preheat the oven to 350°F.
2. Combine the water and millet in a 2-quart saucepan with a tight-fitting lid. Bring to a boil over high heat. Reduce the heat to medium-low, cover the pan, and cook the millet until tender, about 20 minutes.
3. While the millet cooks, sauté the onion in a small skillet over medium-high heat until it turns translucent and starts to brown, about 5 minutes. Add water 1 or 2 tablespoons at a time to keep the onion from sticking to the pan.
4. Add the garlic, sun-dried tomatoes, tamari, sage, fennel, and red pepper flakes, and sauté for another minute to toast the seasonings. Remove the skillet from the heat. Add the nutritional yeast and cooked millet, season with sea salt to taste, and mix well.
5. Using a ¼-cup measure or small ice cream scoop, shape the millet mixture into patties and place them on a nonstick baking sheet or a regular baking sheet lined with parchment paper.
6. Bake for 15 minutes, turn over the patties, and continue to bake until the patties are firm to the touch and lightly browned, another 10 minutes or so. Serve warm.

NOTE FOR THE COOK

For the millet to work as a binder to hold everything together in these patties, you need to almost overcook it. If it seems crumbly when you first make it, add 2 to 3 tablespoons more water to the pan, cover tightly, and let it cook for another 2 to 3 minutes. The millet should hold together when pinched between your fingers or pressed against the side of the pan.

SAUSAGE GRAVY

My mom often made some version of biscuits and sausage gravy because it came together so quickly, and we kids loved it. This plant-based recipe is full of flavor and makes a hearty breakfast for the whole family.

Serves 4 to 6

2 tablespoons raw cashews

2 tablespoons whole wheat pastry flour

1 (12-ounce) bag frozen cauliflower or 2 cups fresh cauliflower florets

Sea salt and black pepper

1 recipe Spicy Breakfast Patties (page 56), crumbled

1 recipe Biscuits (page 50)

1. Preheat the oven to 350°F.
2. Spread out the cashews on a small baking sheet and toast them in the oven for 5 minutes. Sprinkle the flour on the sheet and toast until the cashews and flour are lightly browned, another 5 minutes or so.
3. Meanwhile, put the cauliflower in a medium saucepan and add water almost to cover. Bring to a boil over medium-high heat and cook the cauliflower until very tender, 8 to 10 minutes.
4. Using a slotted spoon, transfer the cauliflower to a blender and puree with just enough of the cooking water to make a smooth, creamy mixture.
5. Using a bench scraper or flat-sided spatula, scrape the toasted cashews and flour into the blender with the cauliflower. Season with sea salt and black pepper to taste, and continue to puree until smooth and creamy. Add more of the cooking water from the cauliflower as needed to achieve a gravy-like consistency.
6. Pour the cauliflower mixture into a large saucepan and add the crumbled breakfast patties. Cook over medium heat until warmed through, about 5 minutes.
7. To serve, split the biscuits in half and place one or two on each plate. Spoon the gravy over the biscuits.

📝 NOTE FOR THE COOK

When toasting nuts and flours, be aware that they go from delicious to burned very quickly. Set your timer and stay close to the oven so you can keep an eye on them.

CHORIZO HASH

I never liked sweet potatoes growing up unless they were in a casserole covered with marshmallows. And I had never had chorizo until a friend invited me over for brunch one Sunday and served a version of this dish. It was a favorite of her children, who eagerly gobbled it down and asked for more. I asked for more, too. This dish is a good one to let the family help with chopping and measuring, preferably on a lazy weekend morning.

Serves 6 to 8

1 medium yellow onion, diced

1 large red bell pepper, seeded and diced

3 garlic cloves, minced

1 teaspoon ancho chile powder

½ teaspoon ground cinnamon

½ teaspoon ground cumin

¼ teaspoon ground allspice

1 large sweet potato, peeled and diced

1 (10-ounce) bag frozen corn (about 1½ cups)

1 recipe Chorizo (page 62), coarsely crumbled

Grated zest and juice of 1 lime

Sea salt and black pepper

1. Sauté the onion and bell pepper in a large saucepan over medium heat until the onion turns translucent and starts to brown, about 8 minutes. Add water 1 or 2 tablespoons at a time to keep the vegetables from sticking to the pan.
2. Add the garlic, chile powder, cinnamon, cumin, and allspice, and cook for another minute.
3. Add the sweet potato and corn and sauté until tender, about 10 minutes.
4. Add the crumbled chorizo, lime zest, and lime juice to the pan; season with sea salt and black pepper to taste; and cook until heated through, about 5 minutes. Serve warm.

CHORIZO

This healthy version of the traditional Mexican sausage makes a tasty side dish for your favorite brunch, and it's a great way to introduce your kids to foods from another culture. Make it for the Chorizo Hash recipe (page 61) or Breakfast Tacos (page 64).

Makes 14 to 16 patties

2½ cups water

1¼ cups millet

1 tablespoon apple cider vinegar

3 garlic cloves, minced

1 teaspoon dried Mexican oregano

1 teaspoon ancho chile powder

½ teaspoon smoked paprika

½ teaspoon black pepper

½ teaspoon ground cumin

Pinch ground allspice

Sea salt, to taste

1. Preheat the oven to 350°F (or 425°F if you plan to serve these as patties).
2. Combine the water and millet in a 2-quart saucepan with a tight-fitting lid. Bring to a boil over high heat. Reduce the heat to medium-low, cover the pan, and cook the millet until tender, about 20 minutes. Add all the remaining ingredients and mix well.
3. Using a ¼-cup measure or small ice cream scoop, shape the millet mixture into patties and place them on a nonstick baking sheet or a regular baking sheet lined with parchment paper. (If you will not be using all the patties right away, stack them between sheets of waxed paper and pack them into a zip-top bag. Freeze for up to 1 month.)
4. If you will be using the chorizo to make hash or tacos, bake the patties at 350°F until lightly browned, about 15 minutes. Turn the patties over and continue to bake for another 10 minutes. If you will be serving these as

patties, bake for 10 minutes at 425°F, turn them over, and then bake another 10 minutes.

📝 NOTE FOR THE COOK

For the millet to work as a binder in this dish (to hold everything together in a patty), you need to almost overcook it. If it seems crumbly when you first make it, add 2 to 3 tablespoons more water to the pan, cover tightly, and let it cook for another 2 to 3 minutes. The millet should hold together when pinched between your fingers or pressed against the side of the pan.

BREAKFAST TACOS

Tacos are a great family meal—even for breakfast!—because everyone can make their tacos to suit their own taste. If you keep all the ingredients on hand and prepped, kids can make this healthy meal any time of day with little or no supervision.

Serves 4

12 to 16 small corn tortillas

1 recipe Spicy Breakfast Patties (page 56) or Chorizo (page 62), crumbled, kept warm

1 large tomato, chopped

1 large red onion, sliced thin and chopped

2 cups shredded romaine lettuce

1 large ripe avocado, pitted, peeled, and sliced

1½ cups favorite salsa

1. Heat a large nonstick skillet over medium heat for 5 minutes. Arrange enough tortillas to cover the bottom of the pan and heat them for 3 to 4 minutes. Turn and heat the other side for 2 minutes. Do not let the tortillas toast for too long or they will become stiff. Heat the remaining tortillas in the same way.

2. To serve the tacos, spoon some of the crumbled breakfast patties down the center of each tortilla, then top with some of the tomato, red onion, lettuce, avocado, and salsa. Fold the tortilla over the filling and serve.

🍽 RECIPE TIP

Set up all the ingredients on the table and let each person make their own tacos. That way everyone can make them to their own preference.

ASPARAGUS, LEEK, AND MUSHROOM FRITTATA

Frittatas are basically crustless quiches and can be an easy, delicious breakfast, brunch, or dinner. Let the kids choose their favorite vegetables for this dish so they can feel a part of the menu-planning process.

Serves 4

1 large leek, light green and white parts, finely chopped

2 cups sliced button mushrooms

2 cups chopped asparagus (½-inch pieces)

4 garlic cloves, minced

1 teaspoon dried thyme

Sea salt and black pepper

1 (12-ounce) package extra-firm silken tofu

¼ cup chickpea flour

2 tablespoons nutritional yeast

¼ teaspoon ground nutmeg

1. In a large skillet, sauté the leek and mushrooms over medium-high heat until the vegetables start to brown, about 5 minutes. Add water 1 or 2 tablespoons at a time to keep the vegetables from sticking to the pan.

2. Add the asparagus and sauté for another 3 minutes. Add the garlic and thyme and sauté for 1 minute more. Season the vegetables with sea salt and black pepper to taste and remove from the heat.

3. Combine the silken tofu, chickpea flour, nutritional yeast, and nutmeg in a food processor; season with sea salt and black pepper to taste; and process until smooth.

4. Transfer the tofu mixture to the pan with the vegetables and mix well. Pour the mixture into a nonstick 9-inch pie pan or nonstick 8-inch square baking dish. Bake until the frittata is set, 40 to 45 minutes.

5. Allow to stand for 10 minutes before slicing.

🍲 RECIPE TIP

If you want to make this frittata with different vegetables, remember that the key to making successful substitutions in most recipes is to replace each ingredient with an equal amount of another. So, if you want to use broccoli instead of asparagus in this dish, use 2 cups chopped broccoli florets.

📝 NOTE FOR THE COOK

Substituting different herbs and spices can be a little tricky. One herb may have a stronger flavor than another, so substituting a similar amount may have vastly different results in flavor. Start small when making substitutions until you know how each herb or spice will affect your final dish. Let the student-cooks in your kitchen smell and taste different herbs, and talk to them about making simple substitutions in a recipe until they develop the confidence to attempt a major recipe overhaul.

BREAKFAST SANDWICH

Because my mom worked, we usually had little time for fancy breakfasts during the week, but before Dad picked us up on the weekend, she would sometimes make something more complicated like this on-the-go breakfast sandwich. (I think she was trying to show Dad that she was still the better cook.) These sandwiches don't have to be a weekend treat: if you make the components ahead of time, you can send your family off to work and school on Monday with this healthy, filling breakfast in hand.

Makes 8 sandwiches

8 Biscuits (page 50)
8 Spicy Breakfast Patties (page 56)
1 recipe Asparagus, Leek, and Mushroom Frittata (page 66), cut into 8 slices
Mayonnaise (page 97)

Split each biscuit in half. Place a patty on the bottom half of each biscuit, top it with a slice of the frittata, and add a dollop of mayonnaise. Cover with the other half of the biscuit and serve.

BIG, FAT BREAKFAST BURRITO

My great-grandfather Harry used to mash together everything on his breakfast plate before he ate it. The first time I ate a breakfast burrito in one of my favorite local cafes, it made me think of him. Burritos make a great family breakfast because, like with breakfast tacos, kids can assemble their own to their taste.

Makes 4 burritos

1 large yellow onion, diced

1 large red bell pepper, seeded and diced

4 garlic cloves, minced

2 teaspoons ground cumin

1 pound fresh baby spinach or 1 (12-ounce) package
   frozen spinach, thawed and wrung dry

¼ cup water

Sea salt and black pepper

1 recipe Breakfast Potatoes (page 54)

1 recipe Spicy Breakfast Patties (page 56), crumbled

4 large whole-grain lavash or large tortillas

1 recipe Queso Sauce (page 100), heated

Chopped scallions, for garnish

Chopped fresh cilantro, for garnish

1. Sauté the onion and bell pepper in a large saucepan over medium heat until the onion turns translucent and starts to brown, about 8 minutes. Add water 1 or 2 tablespoons at a time to keep the vegetables from sticking. Add the garlic and cumin and cook for another minute.

2. Add the spinach and water. Season the vegetables with sea salt and black pepper to taste, cover the pan, and cook until the spinach wilts, about 3 minutes. Remove the pan from the heat. Stir in the potatoes and crumbled breakfast patties.

3. Spread out the lavash on a work surface and divide the filling evenly among them. Fold the lavash over from the sides to the center and then roll the burritos up.

4. To serve, place one burrito on each plate and spoon some sauce over the top. Garnish with the chopped scallions and cilantro.

📝 NOTE FOR THE COOK

This recipe uses three other recipes from the book, offering a good opportunity to teach the new cooks in the house about menu planning and cross-purposing different recipes to use in more than one way. When I plan my menu for the week, I think of recipes like this one where I can make a double batch of some ingredients, such as Queso Sauce, to use in a few different recipes.

BREAKFAST CASSEROLE WITH HASH BROWN CRUST

My friend Lisa makes a few casseroles each week to freeze and have on hand when she doesn't have time during the week to cook. She pulls the casserole out of the freezer the night before she wants to bake it and lets it thaw in the refrigerator. If she is coming home late from work, the kids can throw it in the oven and have a healthy dinner. And who doesn't like breakfast for dinner?

Serves 6 to 8

1 (12-ounce) package extra-firm silken tofu

3 tablespoons chickpea flour (see Tip)

2 tablespoons nutritional yeast

¾ teaspoon sea salt, or to taste

Black pepper, to taste

¼ teaspoon ground nutmeg

1 medium yellow onion, thinly sliced

1 red bell pepper, seeded and diced

8 ounces button mushrooms, sliced

4 garlic cloves, minced

1 recipe Spicy Breakfast Patties (page 56), crumbled

1 (12-ounce) package frozen spinach, thawed and wrung dry

2 large russet potatoes, peeled and grated

1. Preheat the oven to 350°F.
2. Combine the silken tofu, chickpea flour, nutritional yeast, sea salt, black pepper, and nutmeg in a blender, and puree until smooth and creamy.
3. In a large skillet, sauté the onion, bell pepper, and mushrooms over medium heat until the onion turns translucent and starts to brown, about 8 minutes. Add water 1 or 2 tablespoons at a time to keep the vegetables from sticking. Add the garlic and sauté for another minute.

4. Remove the skillet from the heat. Add the pureed tofu mixture, crumbled breakfast patties, and spinach and mix well. Pour the mixture into a nonstick 9×13-inch baking dish.
5. Season the potatoes with sea salt and black pepper to taste. Scatter the grated potatoes over the casserole and cover with aluminum foil.
6. Bake for 20 minutes. Remove the foil and continue to bake until the potatoes are browned, 12 to 15 minutes more. Let the casserole sit for 10 minutes before slicing and serving.

🍽 RECIPE TIP

Chickpea flour is a gluten-free flour and is not easily exchanged for flours containing gluten. It's used in this dish as a thickening agent and, while you can use wheat flours instead, chickpea flour imparts a specific flavor that works especially well in this dish.

SAUSAGE GRAVY AND BISCUIT CASSEROLE

Casseroles are a great way to cook ahead for the week, and older kids can throw them in the oven themselves, either for breakfast on hectic mornings or when Mom and Dad are running late for dinner. We didn't have a lot of casseroles for breakfast growing up, but we did have sausage gravy and biscuits. Whenever I woke up and smelled Mom making biscuits from scratch on a Saturday morning, I knew what was coming.

Serves 8

¼ cup raw cashews

1 (12-ounce) bag frozen cauliflower or 2 cups fresh cauliflower florets

1 medium yellow onion, thinly sliced

1 large red bell pepper, seeded and chopped

1 (12-ounce) bag frozen broccoli florets or 2 cups fresh broccoli florets

1 large zucchini, cut into ¾-inch dice

Sea salt and black pepper

1 recipe Spicy Breakfast Patties (page 56), crumbled

1 recipe Biscuits (page 50), unbaked

1. Preheat the oven to 350°F.
2. Spread out the cashews on a small baking sheet and toast them in the oven until lightly browned, about 10 minutes.
3. Meanwhile, put the cauliflower in a medium saucepan and add water almost to cover. Bring to a boil over medium-high heat and cook the cauliflower until very tender, 8 to 10 minutes.
4. Using a slotted spoon, transfer the cauliflower to a blender. Add the cashews. Puree with just enough of the cauliflower cooking water to make a smooth, creamy mixture.
5. In a large saucepan, sauté the onion and bell pepper over medium-high heat until the onion starts to turn translucent, about 6 minutes. Add water 1 or 2 tablespoons at a time to keep the vegetables from sticking to the pan.

6. Add the broccoli, cover the pan, and cook until the broccoli is tender, about 5 minutes. Add the zucchini and let the vegetables cook, covered, for another 2 minutes. Season with sea salt and black pepper to taste.

7. Add the cauliflower puree and crumbled breakfast patties to the pan with the vegetables and mix well. Spoon the mixture into a nonstick 9×13-inch baking dish.

8. Use a medium ice cream scoop or a ⅓-cup measure to form about eight biscuits from the unbaked dough. Top the casserole with the biscuits and bake until the biscuits are browned and firm to the touch, 20 to 25 minutes. Let the casserole sit for 10 minutes before slicing and serving.

📝 NOTE FOR THE COOK

Oil-free baked goods go from done to overdone very quickly. Watch the timer and check the biscuits in the last few minutes of baking. If they feel firm on top, they are done.

📝 NOTE FOR THE COOK

Pureeing cauliflower is one of my favorite ways to make a creamy sauce. The key to a smooth texture is to make sure the cauliflower is well cooked so it is not gritty when pureed, and then to puree it long enough to remove any lumps.

FRENCH TOAST CASSEROLE

French toast always feels like a special treat, but it's not hard to make. Turning it into a casserole is even easier because it bakes in the oven, so you don't have to cook each slice on the stovetop. If your kids have mastered pancakes, French toast can be their next breakfast cooking achievement.

Serves 6 to 8

1 (1-pound) loaf crusty whole-grain bread, cut into 1-inch cubes

1 (12-ounce) package extra-firm silken tofu

4 Medjool dates, pitted

1 cup unsweetened plant milk

½ cup unsweetened applesauce

2 teaspoons pure vanilla extract

¼ cup arrowroot powder

1 teaspoon ground cinnamon

½ teaspoon ground nutmeg

½ teaspoon sea salt

Fresh fruit (such as berries or sliced bananas), for serving (optional)

Pure maple syrup, for serving (optional)

1. Scatter the bread cubes all over the bottom of a nonstick 9×13-inch baking dish.
2. In a food processor, combine the silken tofu, dates, plant milk, applesauce, vanilla, arrowroot powder, cinnamon, nutmeg, and sea salt. Puree the mixture until it is smooth and creamy.
3. Pour the mixture over the bread cubes. Cover the casserole with plastic wrap and refrigerate for at least 2 hours, or overnight.
4. Preheat the oven to 375°F.
5. Remove the plastic wrap and bake the casserole until golden brown, about 40 minutes. Serve warm, with fresh fruit or maple syrup, if desired.

📝 NOTE FOR THE COOK

There are two types of tofu used in cooking. Silken tofu has a creamy texture, making it good for dishes where you want a custard-like texture, such as this one. Chinese-style tofu is the firm kind you are used to seeing sold in blocks, packed in water. This type holds its shape and is better suited for marinating, grilling, and baking. Take the kids shopping and show them how to read labels. It will help them identify healthy foods and distinguish between different types of tofu.

At Home with the Plant-Based Family

PAM POPPER

Dr. Pam Popper is an internationally recognized health, diet, and nutrition expert; co-author of *Food Over Medicine*; and founder of the Wellness Health Forum, an organization offering evidence-based alternatives to the traditional health care model, informed medical decision making, educational programming, and instructional content and training. In her experience, transitioning your family to a plant-based diet is simple; it just takes discipline and patience.

How you handle your children when it comes to changing diets depends on their age. Teenagers will often express more disinterest in or aggravation with the change, but kids aged eight and younger are easier to create healthy habits for.

"When you have a lot of control over the food, you don't negotiate," Pam says. "I don't believe in negotiating with children. This is not meant to be disrespectful to children. They're just not mature enough" to make their own decisions, especially regarding health and nutrition. Children may know what they like to eat, but they don't know enough about nutrition to make healthy decisions.

Pam recommends starting by serving healthier versions of familiar foods, like the Mac and Cheese (page 224), Carrot Dogs (page 150), or Grilled Cheese Sandwiches (page 145) in this book. "I think this can even be a problem for adults where we think that this is all about eating black quinoa and exotic vegetables right off the bat, and that's a surefire way to turn off an eight-year-old. Take some unsweetened brown soy milk and pour it on the children's cereal, and now you've lost them for the rest of your natural days."

Pam also suggests parents let their children try new foods and get them involved in the shopping process to help them get excited about the change. According to Pam, there are two important things to remember when getting young children involved: "waiting for the teachable moments and giving them things that are likely to capture their attention," as well as patience. "Patience is the key," she says.

All of that advice is great for inside the home. What about outside of it? Plant-based meal options are sometimes hard to find in school and work settings, and what your children eat at other families' homes is often out of your control. This is why it's so important to create plant-based habits when children are young; as they get older, they'll be much more likely to choose healthier options no matter where they are.

One of the biggest problems with getting children to eat plant-based fare is school lunches. They tend to be heavy on cheap-to-produce, fried, and sugar- and fat-filled foods, with few vegetables—which is why Pam encourages parents to pack kids a lunch, while pushing for systemic change if possible.

Still, the most important part of implementing a plant-based diet for your child is *your* mindset—and that of your partner. They don't have to be on board them-selves, as long as they support the change in your children's diet. Even if you and your partner are separated or divorced and do not get along, the one thing you should be able to agree on is the welfare of your children. With that com-mon ground, you can work together to create the most consistent and supportive dietary environment possible.

SIDES AND SAUCES

SWEET POTATO HUMMUS

Making hummus at home is easy and far less expensive than buying it in a store, and it allows you to season it exactly the way you prefer. Having hummus on hand means the family can have a quick snack or an easy sandwich any time of day.

Serves 6

4 cups sweet potato puree (see Tip on page 48)

¼ cup tahini

4 garlic cloves, peeled

3 tablespoons fresh lemon juice

1 teaspoon ground cumin

1½ teaspoons sea salt

¼ teaspoon cayenne pepper (optional)

Combine all the ingredients in a food processor and puree until smooth and creamy. Store in an airtight container in the refrigerator for up to a week.

SWEET POTATO CORNBREAD

My dad used to make cornbread every weekend to serve with chili. He never made cornbread with sweet potatoes, but every time I serve it to my young cousins, they love the color the sweet potatoes add to the dish.

Serves 9 to 12

1½ cups cornmeal

1½ cups whole wheat pastry flour

4 teaspoons double-acting baking powder

½ teaspoon sea salt

1 teaspoon ground cinnamon (optional)

2 cups unsweetened plant milk

1½ cups sweet potato puree (see Tip on page 48)

½ cup pure maple syrup (optional)

1. Preheat the oven to 375°F.
2. In a large mixing bowl, whisk together the cornmeal, flour, baking powder, sea salt, and cinnamon (if using).
3. In a small bowl, whisk together the plant milk, sweet potato puree, and maple syrup (if using). Add the sweet potato mixture to the bowl with the flour mixture and use a rubber spatula or wooden spoon to gently fold the ingredients together. Do not overmix or the cornbread will be chewy.
4. Spoon the batter into a nonstick 9×13-inch baking dish and bake until a toothpick inserted into the center of the cornbread comes out clean, about 30 minutes. Let sit for 15 minutes before slicing and serving.

CORN CHIPS

I grew up loving Fritos almost as much as potato chips. But with the current obesity epidemic in the United States, finding tasty snacks not fried in fat is a must for kids—and for their parents, too. Try these with Nachos (page 89) or in a Chilaquiles Frittata (page 190).

Serves 4

12 (6-inch) corn tortillas
Sea salt (optional)

1. Preheat the oven to 350°F.
2. Stack three tortillas on a flat surface and cut them into eight wedges. Repeat with the remaining tortillas. Arrange all the tortilla wedges in a single layer on a baking sheet—you may need to do this in batches or use more than one baking sheet.
3. Bake the chips until crispy, 15 to 20 minutes, checking them for crispness after 10 minutes and then every 3 or 4 minutes. Season with sea salt to taste.
4. Let the chips cool to room temperature, then store them in an airtight container for up to 3 days.

📝 NOTE FOR THE COOK

The key to perfect corn chips is timing. They go from crisp to burned very quickly, so keep your eye on them toward the end of the baking time. These chips will also continue to crisp as they cool.

NACHOS

Nachos are a perennial favorite among kids and adults alike. You can feel good about serving this version, which is not loaded down with oils and goopy dairy cheese like most restaurant nachos. Try them with Corn and Black Bean Salsa (page 126).

Serves 4

1 recipe Corn Chips (page 86)

1 cup Cheese Sauce (page 98) or Queso Sauce (page 100)

1 cup chopped fresh cilantro or scallions

1 cup sliced pickled jalapeño peppers

Favorite salsa (optional)

1. Preheat the broiler to high.
2. Spread out the corn chips on a baking sheet so that they are slightly overlapping and drizzle the sauce over them.
3. Broil until the sauce is bubbly, 4 to 5 minutes. Top with the cilantro and pickled jalapeños. Serve with salsa, if desired.

POTATO WEDGES

Americans think they can stave off obesity in their children (and themselves) by keeping white potatoes off the dinner plate, never understanding that it's the fat in which we fry potatoes and the butter and sour cream we put on top of them that are the real culprits. Welcome white potatoes back to your dinner table with this healthy, tasty recipe.

Serves 4

4 medium to large russet potatoes, scrubbed and cut into ½-inch-thick wedges

½ teaspoon granulated garlic

½ teaspoon granulated onion

½ teaspoon paprika

½ teaspoon black pepper

Sea salt, to taste

1. Preheat the oven to 350°F. Line a rimmed baking sheet with parchment paper.
2. Put the potato wedges in a bowl and toss with the seasonings. Arrange the potatoes in a single layer on the lined baking sheet.
3. Bake until the potatoes are lightly browned and crisp, 20 to 25 minutes.

🗒 NOTE FOR THE COOK

The key to cutting potatoes safely is carefully cutting them in half so that they sit with stability on the work surface, and then cutting each half as you wish.

TATER TOTS

I loved tater tots when I was a kid but gave them up when I quit eating fried foods—too much oil. This version is my new favorite. They are flavorful, perfectly crisped, and delicious. Your kids (or the kid in you) can eat them with abandon.

Serves 4

2 pounds Yukon gold potatoes, peeled

1 tablespoon arrowroot powder

2 teaspoons sea salt, or to taste

2 teaspoons granulated onion

2 teaspoons granulated garlic

1. Put the potatoes in a large pot. Cover with water and bring to a boil over high heat. Reduce the heat to medium, cover the pot, and let the potatoes cook until tender when poked with a fork, 15 to 20 minutes. Drain the potatoes and set aside until cool enough to handle.
2. Preheat the oven to 450°F.
3. Grate the potatoes into a bowl using the largest holes on a box grater. Add the arrowroot powder, sea salt, granulated onion, and granulated garlic, and gently mix until well combined.
4. Form the grated potato mixture into tater tot shapes and place them in a single layer on a nonstick rimmed baking sheet. Bake for 15 minutes, then flip the tater tots and bake for another 12 to 15 minutes, until they are browned and crispy.

📝 NOTE FOR THE COOK

Undercooked potatoes made without oil will not brown. Overcook them and they become too chewy. When baking any dish, check for the finished product at the early end of the cooking time—in this case, at 20 minutes—then check every 5 minutes until the potatoes are perfectly browned.

SOUR CREAM

The first time I served this healthy nondairy version of sour cream to kids in one of my cooking classes, they did not know it wasn't the real thing. I call that health by deception.

Makes 1½ cups

1 (12-ounce) package extra-firm silken tofu

2 tablespoons rice vinegar

2 tablespoons toasted pine nuts (see Note on page 43; optional)

Pinch sea salt

Combine all the ingredients in a food processor and puree until smooth and creamy.

 RECIPE TIP

Make sure to puree the sour cream long enough to get rid of all lumps. You may need to use a spatula to push down the sides of the mixture to get everything pureed. Store the sour cream in an airtight container in the refrigerator for up to 7 days.

MAYONNAISE

I've never been able to find a commercial mayonnaise made without oil, so I created this recipe. If you don't tell your family, they may not guess that this mayonnaise is made from tofu. They will just happily use it on all their favorite sandwiches.

Makes 1½ cups

1 (12-ounce) package extra-firm silken tofu

3 tablespoons red wine vinegar or rice vinegar

2 teaspoons nutritional yeast

1 teaspoon mustard powder

1 teaspoon granulated onion

1 teaspoon granulated garlic

½ teaspoon sea salt, or to taste

Combine all the ingredients in a blender and puree until smooth and creamy, about 2 minutes. Store the mayonnaise in an airtight container in the refrigerator for up to 7 days.

 RECIPE TIP

Be sure to puree the mayonnaise long enough to get rid of all lumps. You may need to use a spatula to push down the sides of the mixture to get everything pureed.

CHEESE SAUCE

Kids love anything made with cheese, which is, unfortunately, the least healthy food on the planet. I've fed this plant-based "cheese" sauce to kids and grown-ups alike who did not know they were eating a sauce made from potatoes. This versatile recipe can be used in Nachos (page 89), Mac and Cheese (page 224), or even a Grilled Cheese Sandwich (page 145).

Makes about 2½ cups

1½ cups finely diced russet potatoes (about 1 medium potato)

¼ cup finely diced red bell pepper

½ small yellow onion, diced

2 tablespoons raw cashews

2 tablespoons tahini

1 tablespoon fresh lemon juice

2 tablespoons nutritional yeast

2 tablespoons arrowroot powder

1 teaspoon sea salt, or to taste

1. Combine the potato, bell pepper, onion, and cashews in a small saucepan and cover with water. Bring the water to a boil over high heat, reduce the heat to medium, and cook until the potatoes are very tender, about 10 minutes. Drain the vegetables, reserving ¾ cup of the cooking water.
2. Combine the potato mixture, reserved cooking water, tahini, lemon juice, nutritional yeast, arrowroot powder, and sea salt in a blender. Process on high until everything is smooth and creamy, about 3 minutes. Store the sauce in an airtight container in the refrigerator for up to 5 days.

📝 NOTE FOR THE COOK

The key to cutting potatoes safely is carefully cutting them in half so that they sit with stability on the work surface, and then cutting each half as you wish.

📝 NOTE FOR THE COOK

The secret to a creamy cheese sauce is in making sure the potatoes are well cooked (they should be very tender when poked with a fork), and then pureeing the potato mixture for several minutes to break down the starch in the potatoes.

QUESO SAUCE

This cheese sauce is not only healthy but also tastes great as a dip for Corn Chips (page 86) or cut-up veggies.

Makes about 2½ cups

1½ cups finely diced russet potatoes (about 1 medium potato)

½ small yellow onion, diced

2 tablespoons raw cashews

2 tablespoons chopped green chiles

¼ cup finely chopped fresh cilantro

¼ cup finely chopped scallion

2 tablespoons tahini

1 tablespoon fresh lemon juice

2 tablespoons nutritional yeast

2 tablespoons arrowroot powder

1 teaspoon sea salt, or to taste

1. Combine the potato, onion, and cashews in a small saucepan, and cover with water. Bring the water to a boil over high heat, reduce the heat to medium, and cook until the potatoes are very tender, about 10 minutes. Drain the vegetables, reserving ¾ cup of the cooking water.
2. Combine the potato mixture, reserved cooking water, green chiles, cilantro, scallion, tahini, lemon juice, nutritional yeast, arrowroot powder, and sea salt in a blender. Process on high speed until everything is smooth and creamy, about 3 minutes. Store the sauce in an airtight container in the refrigerator for up to 5 days.

📝 NOTE FOR THE COOK

The key to cutting potatoes safely is carefully cutting them in half so that they sit with stability on the work surface, and then cutting each half as you wish.

 **NOTE FOR THE COOK**

The secret to a creamy cheese sauce is in making sure the potatoes are well cooked (they should be very tender when poked with a fork), and then pureeing the potato mixture for several minutes to break down the starch in the potatoes.

GOOD GRAVY

As a kid, I liked mashed potatoes only because they acted as a bowl for the gravy. This is one of my favorite gravies, and I put it on everything from mashed potatoes to brown rice.

Makes about 4 cups

1½ cups low-sodium vegetable broth

1 (15-ounce) can white beans, rinsed and drained, or 1½ cups cooked white beans (see Tip)

8 ounces button mushrooms, sliced

1 medium yellow onion, diced

3 garlic cloves, minced

1 teaspoon dried thyme

Black pepper

3 tablespoons tamari, or to taste

1 tablespoon pure maple syrup

1 tablespoon apple cider vinegar

1. Combine the vegetable broth and white beans in a blender and puree until smooth and creamy. Set aside.
2. In a large skillet, sauté the mushrooms and onion over medium-high heat until the onion starts to brown and turn translucent, about 5 minutes. Add water 1 or 2 tablespoons at a time to keep the vegetables from sticking to the pan. Add the garlic, thyme, and black pepper to taste, and sauté for 1 minute.
3. Add the white bean mixture, tamari, maple syrup, and apple cider vinegar; bring the mixture to a boil; and cook, stirring occasionally, until the gravy is reduced and thickens slightly, about 10 minutes. Store the gravy in an airtight container in the refrigerator for up to 5 days.

 RECIPE TIP

Any white beans will work in this recipe—Great Northern, cannellini, or navy—so use whatever you have on hand.

 **RECIPE TIP**

Gravy is traditionally thickened with a starch, like flour, cornstarch, or arrowroot powder. This one uses beans (which, by the way, have a starch in them). The secret to a creamy, lump-free gravy is to make sure you puree the beans long enough.

SEVEN-LAYER DIP

This dip is very popular at parties for kids of any age. It's not only pretty to look at but also fun to eat. This version is just as healthy as it is tasty.

Serves 6 to 8

1 (15-ounce) can fat-free vegan refried beans

¼ cup water

1 (16-ounce) jar salsa

1 recipe Queso Sauce (page 100)

1 large tomato, chopped

1½ cups sliced black olives

4 scallions, thinly sliced

1 cup chopped fresh cilantro

1 recipe Corn Chips (page 86), for serving

In a small bowl, whisk together the refried beans and water to make a creamy mixture. Spread the bean mixture in the bottom of a large glass bowl. Layer the remaining ingredients in the order given, making sure that each layer (especially the salsa and queso) completely covers the layer underneath. Serve with the corn chips on the side for dipping.

 RECIPE TIP

This dip is meant to be layered in a clear bowl so that if you look at the side of the bowl you can see each individual layer. Here's a good opportunity for older children to practice their presentation and plating skills.

BROWN RICE

I find it useful to always have a pot of rice on hand for different dishes. This basic recipe can be used in any number of ways—as a side dish, as a filling for burritos, as the base for a hearty stew, or even as a breakfast cereal with a little warm plant milk, chopped dates, and cinnamon.

Makes 4 cups

2 cups brown rice
4 cups water

Combine the rice and water in a 2-quart saucepan, cover, and bring the water to a boil over high heat. Reduce the heat to medium-low and let it simmer for 45 minutes, or until the water is absorbed and the rice is tender.

📝 NOTE FOR THE COOK

The key to cooking any grain is to make sure to leave the lid on for the entire cooking time. Uncovering the pan before the end of the cooking time will release steam, and then you will not have enough liquid left to fully cook the grain.

📝 NOTE FOR THE COOK

When a recipe calls for you to *simmer* a dish, it means to cook it at just below the boiling point, with the liquid barely moving in the pan.

MILLET

Teaching your kids about the origins of foods is a great way to talk about geography. Millet is a cereal grass grown by humans for thousands of years and is a staple grain from Asia to Africa. In the United States, it is grown more for bird food than for human consumption. It has a mild nutty flavor and cooks quickly.

Makes 2½ cups

1 cup millet
2 cups water

Combine the millet and water in a 2-quart saucepan, cover, and bring the water to a boil over high heat. Reduce the heat to medium-low and let it simmer for 20 minutes.

RECIPE TIP

This recipe is for millet that can be used in dishes that require it to be formed into patties or loaves, so it needs to be slightly overcooked. Check the millet after 20 minutes—not before—by removing the lid and looking at the grains to see if any of them are still tight little seeds. Fully cooked millet should be fluffy.

NOTE FOR THE COOK

The key to cooking any grain is to make sure to leave the lid on for the entire cooking time. Uncovering the pan before the end of the cooking time will release steam, and then you will not have enough liquid left to fully cook the grain.

NOTE FOR THE COOK

When a recipe calls for you to *simmer* a dish, it means to cook it at just below the boiling point, with the liquid barely moving in the pan.

QUINOA

When I teach cooking classes for kids, I like to talk to them about unusual foods like quinoa. When you talk to them about where it was originally from, you teach them about geography. When you talk to them about how to prepare it, you teach them how easy cooking can be. And when you talk to them about all the ways you can use this nutty-flavored grain, you teach them about versatility—all good lessons.

Makes 3 cups

1½ cups quinoa, rinsed under cool water

3 cups water

Combine the quinoa and water in a 2-quart saucepan, cover, and bring the water to a boil over high heat. Reduce the heat to medium-low and let it simmer for 20 minutes, until the water is absorbed and the quinoa is tender.

📝 NOTE FOR THE COOK

The key to cooking any grain is to make sure to leave the lid on for the entire cooking time. Taking the lid off of the pan before the end of the cooking time will release steam, and then you will not have enough liquid left to fully cook the grain.

📝 NOTE FOR THE COOK

When a recipe calls for you to *simmer* a dish, it means to cook it at just below the boiling point, with the liquid barely moving in the pan.

🍽 RECIPE TIP

Quinoa contains a compound, known as a saponin, that acts as a natural pesticide to protect the grain from birds and other prey. That saponin can make the quinoa taste bitter. Many manufacturers now remove the saponin before packaging the grain, but if you find that your quinoa tastes bitter, it may need an additional rinse before cooking.

At Home with the Plant-Based Family

LUANN HOOVER

Luann Hoover is not only an employee at my and Pam Popper's organization, Wellness Forum Health, but also a close friend. Her journey toward a plant-based diet, undertaken before we met, started where many do: in a doctor's office. In for a routine checkup, Luann found out that her cholesterol was high enough that the doctor recommended she go on statins. With a family history of high cholesterol and blood pressure, Luann was not shocked, but she was disappointed. Luann had always tried to avoid pharmaceuticals, an opinion formed after years of taking care of her autistic daughter.

After having tried many different conventional treatments for her daughter's gastrointestinal issues, Luann found alternative/natural interventions proved the most effective. "The whole autism puzzle that I've been trying to solve, to help improve my daughter's physical obstacles, really fine-tuned my belief that when we have a physical problem the best way to treat it is to figure out the origin," not simply rely on various pharmaceutical drugs.

Shortly after that doctor's appointment, she had an appointment with her optometrist, who asked her if she took any medication.

"I said, 'No, but I am supposed to go on statins.' My optometrist told me that she has a few friends who had high cholesterol and they adopted a vegan diet. It supposedly lowers the cholesterol," says Luann. She immediately started researching the diet, starting with *Preventing and Reversing Heart Disease* by Caldwell Esselstyn and ending with *The China Study* by T. Colin Campbell and Thomas M. Campbell. She became a vegan the following week, determined to avoid going on statins. The decision to switch diets was simple because she had always wanted to be vegetarian and her health was a key motivational factor.

"*The China Study* was the thing that really just energized my decision because of its focus on cancer and other diseases. I wanted to make sure that I was healthy so that I will live as long as I can to help my daughter," she says.

After making the change, Luann never looked back. "I had always wanted to be vegetarian, but my family is not vegetarian. I didn't want to inconvenience people. I didn't want to cause problems. Now I had an excuse, and so I did it."

Happily, her new diet was met with little resistance and a lot of enthusiasm. Her husband read *The China Study* and became a vegan as well. Even her daughter got on the plant-based diet bandwagon.

The biggest hurdle to overcome? Her daughter Isabel's love of dairy. However, Luann suspected this love was exactly what was fogging her mind and convinced her to try a vegan cheese recipe with cashews, nutritional yeast, onion powder, garlic powder, and salt. "She now makes it independently, on her own every week," Luann says. "She has always been foggy and spaced out. She's improved with other interventions, but when we adopted the vegan diet, even her occupational therapist noticed the difference. She's been treating my daughter since she was three, and my daughter is fifteen now. She asked me about a month or two in, 'Have you done something different with Isabel?'"

Isabel experienced significant improvement in her visual, motor, spatial, and cognitive functions—greater improvements than from any previous intervention. "I find that a lot of kids on the spectrum have difficulty paying attention, attending, keeping their attention. I believe that dairy is the number one cause of the fog."

Luann's thirteen-year-old son recently also decided to become vegan. When he asked Luann how he could grow as tall as possible and be as athletic as possible, she told him he needs to eat foods that are high in nutrition: fruits, vegetables, and whole grains. Because he was learning about making good food choices in his health class at school, he was more open to this information than he had been in the past. He changed from being anti-fruit and -vegetable and pro–fast food to pro-fruit and -vegetable and anti–fast food!

Between the improvement in her and her daughter's health and the enthusiastic participation of her husband and son, eating plant-based has given Luann hope that she will not only be healthy herself in years to come, but also have a healthy family to take care of.

SALADS AND SALAD FIXINGS

WHITE BEAN "BUTTERMILK" DRESSING

You can serve this dressing to even the most finicky eater of any age and get a clean plate every time.

Makes 1 cup

1 cup extra-firm silken tofu or 1 cup cooked or canned white beans (see Tip)

¼ cup water, or more if needed

3 tablespoons chopped fresh chives

2 tablespoons fresh lemon juice

1 garlic clove, peeled

1 teaspoon dried dill (see Tip)
½ teaspoon sea salt
Pinch black pepper

_____

Combine all the ingredients in a blender and puree until smooth and creamy. Add more water if necessary to make a pourable dressing.

 ## RECIPE TIP

Any white beans will work in this recipe—Great Northern, cannellini, or navy—so use whatever you have on hand.

 ## NOTE FOR THE COOK

Whether you use the silken tofu or white beans, it is important to puree the mixture well to get a smooth and creamy texture.

 ## NOTE FOR THE COOK

Don't be shy about tasting the dressing before you serve it to make sure you have included all the ingredients. With practice you can tell whether you forgot the sea salt, lemon juice, or chives. Practice makes perfect.

 ## RECIPE TIP

If you have fresh dill on hand, use that instead of the dried dill. When using fresh herbs in place of dried, you'll need three times the amount called for in the recipe. So, for this recipe, you'll need 3 teaspoons, or 1 tablespoon, chopped fresh dill.

GREEN GODDESS DRESSING

The first time I had this dressing, it was from a jar. I liked it well enough, but when I tried a homemade version for the first time, I fell in love with it. Your kids will love the fresh flavor and bright green color.

Makes 1¾ cups

1 (12-ounce) package extra-firm silken tofu, or 1 (15-ounce) can white beans, rinsed and drained, or 1½ cups cooked white beans (see Tip)

¼ cup chopped fresh parsley

2 tablespoons white wine vinegar

2 tablespoons minced yellow onion

2 tablespoons chopped scallion

1 teaspoon dried tarragon

½ teaspoon sea salt

Combine all the ingredients in a food processor. Puree until smooth and creamy. Transfer to a container, cover, and chill for 1 hour before serving.

 RECIPE TIP

Any white beans will work in this recipe—Great Northern, cannellini, or navy—so use whatever you have on hand.

 NOTE FOR THE COOK

Whether you use the silken tofu or white beans, it is important to puree the mixture well to get a smooth and creamy texture.

THOUSAND ISLAND DRESSING

A classic Reuben is one of my favorite sandwiches, but these days I make it with this healthiest of dressings and a marinated portobello mushroom (see the recipe on page 196) instead of the meat- and cheese-laden version of my childhood.

Makes about 2 cups

1 (12-ounce) package extra-firm silken tofu, or 1 (15-ounce) can white beans, rinsed and drained, or 1½ cups cooked white beans (see Tip)

4 dates, pitted

1 garlic clove, minced

¼ cup red wine vinegar

¼ cup tomato puree

1 teaspoon prepared horseradish

½ teaspoon tamari

½ teaspoon mustard powder

½ teaspoon paprika

Combine the tofu and dates in a blender and process until smooth and creamy. Add the remaining ingredients and puree to mix well.

 RECIPE TIP

Any white beans will work in this recipe—Great Northern, cannellini, or navy—so use whatever you have on hand.

 NOTE FOR THE COOK

Whether you use the silken tofu or white beans, it is important to puree the mixture well to get a smooth and creamy texture.

CAESAR SALAD DRESSING

If you think you need to give up Caesar salad because the dressing contains raw eggs, this egg-free recipe will be a pleasant surprise. Most kids love Caesar salad because of the croutons—see page 123 for an easy recipe for homemade croutons.

Makes about 2 cups

1 (15-ounce) can white beans, rinsed and drained, or 1½ cups cooked white beans (see Tip)
½ cup water, or more as needed
2 tablespoons tahini
2 tablespoons fresh lemon juice
1 tablespoon sweet white miso
2 garlic cloves, peeled
2 tablespoons nutritional yeast
1 tablespoon drained capers
1 teaspoon sea salt, or to taste

Combine all the ingredients in a blender and puree until smooth and creamy. Add more water as necessary to get a pourable consistency.

 RECIPE TIP

Any white beans will work in this recipe—Great Northern, cannellini, or navy—so use whatever you have on hand.

 NOTE FOR THE COOK

The trick for making a creamy dressing using beans is to start out with beans that are tender (if you are cooking them from scratch, make sure they are well cooked), and then puree the dressing in a blender for several minutes.

MUSHROOM "BACON"

My mom made BLTs often when we were kids. They were a quick, easy, and inexpensive meal, and we loved them. Try this "bacon" on salads or veggie burgers or to make a healthier BLT for your own kids. They add a lot of flavor however you use them.

Serves 4

3 tablespoons tamari

3 tablespoons pure maple syrup

1 garlic clove, minced

½ teaspoon ground ginger

Black pepper

8 ounces portobello mushrooms, stems removed, caps thinly sliced

1. In a medium-size bowl, whisk together the tamari, maple syrup, garlic, ginger, and black pepper to taste. Add the mushrooms and toss to mix well. Let the mushrooms marinate at room temperature for 1 hour.
2. Preheat a skillet over medium-high heat for 1 minute. Remove the mushrooms from the marinade (but reserve the marinade) and cook them on one side for 2 minutes. Turn them over and cook the other side until they start to brown, another 2 minutes or so.
3. Pour the marinade into the skillet and let it cook briefly, until almost all of it has evaporated. Remove the pan from the heat. The mushrooms will crisp a little as they cool. Serve, or store in an airtight container in the refrigerator for up to 3 days.

CROUTONS

Store-bought croutons are full of unnecessary fat, and most recipes for home-made croutons are just as bad. Your family won't miss all that fat—in fact, these croutons will be so popular you'll want to make extra for snacking.

Makes 2 cups

2 cups cubed whole-grain bread (½-inch cubes)

¼ cup water

2 teaspoons granulated garlic

2 teaspoons granulated onion

1 teaspoon paprika

½ teaspoon sea salt (optional)

1. Preheat the oven to 350°F.
2. Combine all the ingredients in a bowl and toss to mix well. Spread out the croutons in a single layer on a rimmed baking sheet and bake until they are toasted and lightly browned, about 15 minutes. Let cool to room temperature before storing in an airtight container.

GREEN GODDESS SLAW

Slaw makes a great side-dish salad but also dresses up sandwiches very nicely. I especially love this slaw on Mediterranean "Meatball" Subs (page 158) and on Carrot Dogs (page 150). Serve it in place of the usual mayo-heavy slaw and you will be the popular kid at the potluck table.

Serves 4

1 (6-ounce) package slaw mix or 4 cups shredded cabbage

2 scallions, minced

4 fresh basil leaves, minced

½ cup Green Goddess Dressing (page 116), more or less to taste

In a medium-size bowl, toss together the slaw mix, scallions, basil, and dressing until well combined. Cover and let sit (chilling is optional) for 1 hour to allow the flavors to marry.

📝 NOTE FOR THE COOK

Shredding your own cabbage is cheaper than buying prepared slaw mix. You can shred cabbage for slaw using the shredder blade attachment for the food processor or with the large holes of a box grater.

CORN AND BLACK BEAN SALSA

Older kids who have good knife skills can make this recipe on their own to have for a healthy snack. Even younger kids can toss everything together once it has all been cut up.

Serves 6 to 8

2 (15-ounce) cans black beans, rinsed and drained, or 3 cups cooked black beans

1 (12-ounce) bag frozen corn, thawed, or 2 cups fresh corn

2 roasted red bell peppers, diced (see Tip)

1 large tomato, diced

1 small red onion, diced

1 jalapeño pepper, seeded and minced

3 garlic cloves, minced

½ cup chopped fresh cilantro

Grated zest of 1 lime

Juice of 2 limes

2 teaspoons ground cumin

Sea salt, to taste

Combine all the ingredients in a large bowl and mix well. Store in an airtight container in the refrigerator for up to 4 days.

 RECIPE TIP

Serve this salsa with Corn Chips (page 86) as an appetizer or snack, as a salad on a bed of mixed greens, or in a whole-grain tortilla as a wrap.

 NOTE FOR THE COOK

You can buy roasted red peppers in a jar, or you can roast your own. Carefully hold a red bell pepper over an open flame and let it char all over. Transfer it to a paper or plastic bag to steam, then peel off the blackened part by hand. Do not rinse it or you will lose all the flavor of roasting.

AT-HOME SALAD BAR

Restaurant salad bars are popular because everyone can make a salad to their own taste. Having a salad bar at home can give your family the same freedom without breaking the bank.

Here's a guide to creating an at-home salad bar. Stock up on the items your family loves and watch them stock up on salad at the table. Once you have all the ingredients prepped and ready to go, kids of all ages can make their own salad without much adult supervision.

GREENS

Arugula

Baby beet greens

Boston lettuce

Butter lettuce

Endive

Frisée

Mâche

Microgreens

Oak leaf lettuce

Radicchio

Red and green leaf lettuce

Red cabbage

Romaine lettuce

Spinach

Tatsoi

Watercress

FRESH RAW VEGETABLES

Bell peppers

Broccoli

Carrots

Celery

Corn

Cucumbers

Fennel

Mushrooms

Onions

Sprouts (alfalfa, broccoli, mung, etc.)

Sugar snap peas

Tomatoes

Zucchini

COOKED OR STEAMED VEGETABLES

Beets

Potatoes

COOKED OR CANNED BEANS AND LEGUMES

Adzuki beans

Black beans

Chickpeas

Lentils

Pinto beans

Red kidney beans

White beans (Great Northern, cannellini, or navy)

NUTS AND SEEDS

Almonds

Pecans

Pumpkin seeds

Sesame seeds

Sunflower seeds

Walnuts

COOKED OR SPROUTED GRAINS

Amaranth

Brown rice

Millet

Quinoa

Wheat berries

FRESH HERBS

Basil

Cilantro

Oregano

Tarragon

VINEGARS AND SALAD DRESSINGS

Balsamic vinegar

Red wine vinegar

Rice vinegar

Caesar Salad Dressing (page 120)

Green Goddess Dressing (page 116)

Mayonnaise (page 97)

Thousand Island Dressing (page 119)

CAESAR SALAD

If your children are into history, you might teach them the origins of this salad, an example of a dish whose name does not fit its history. None of the Caesars in ancient Rome ate this salad. In fact, it was created by an Italian immigrant and restaurant owner in the 1920s by the name of Caesar Cardini. This version, made with none of the eggs, anchovies, oil, or Parmesan cheese used in Cardini's original recipe, has all the flavor and many more health benefits.

Serves 4

1 large head romaine lettuce, cut into 1-inch pieces (6 to 8 cups)

2 cups Croutons (page 123)

½ cup Caesar Salad Dressing (page 120)

Combine the romaine lettuce, croutons, and dressing in a large bowl and mix well.

 RECIPE TIP

Vegetable salads by themselves are not a filling meal. I make this salad a meal by adding 1 cup cooked or canned chickpeas or white beans.

COBB SALAD

Cobb salad is a composed salad, with each ingredient arranged decoratively on the plate. Let kids arrange it in their own way so they can have fun "playing with their food." Even young children can make this on their own if you have all of the ingredients chopped and the salad dressing on hand in the refrigerator.

Serves 4

1 large head romaine lettuce, cut into 1-inch pieces (6 to 8 cups)

1 large ripe tomato, diced

1 cup fresh or frozen (thawed) corn

½ cup cooked or canned chickpeas

½ cup diced avocado

½ cup Mushroom "Bacon" (page 122)

½ cup White Bean "Buttermilk" Dressing (page 114), or to taste

Spread the romaine lettuce on a platter and arrange the tomato, corn, chick-peas, avocado, and mushroom bacon in rows across the top of the lettuce. Serve with the dressing on the side.

WHITE BEAN SALAD WITH APRICOTS AND PISTACHIOS

I was babysitting for a friend's kids once and decided to make a bean salad for lunch. I let the kids pick some of the ingredients, and this is what we came up with. It is still a favorite of mine—and theirs.

Serves 4

2 (15-ounce) cans white beans, rinsed and drained, or 3 cups cooked white beans (see Tip)

1 medium red onion, diced

1 medium red bell pepper, seeded and diced

¾ cup dried unsulfured apricots, chopped

3 tablespoons chopped fresh mint

½ cup toasted pistachios (see Note on page 43)

Grated zest of 1 orange

Juice of 2 oranges

Juice of 1 lemon

½ teaspoon crushed red pepper flakes

Sea salt, to taste

Combine all the ingredients in a large bowl and mix well. Store in an airtight container in the refrigerator for up to 5 days.

 RECIPE TIP

Any white beans will work in this recipe—Great Northern, cannellini, or navy—so use whatever you have on hand.

 RECIPE TIP

You can use this recipe as a template for different bean salads. Try different beans, different dried or fresh fruits, and different herbs like basil, cilantro, or tarragon. If you are not a fan of beans, substitute 4 cups cooked brown rice (page 106) or cooked quinoa (page 108).

 RECIPE TIP

You might be tempted to skip the orange zest in this dish or to use bottled orange juice or lemon juice in place of fresh juice, but the fresh juice has much better flavor than the bottled. Have fun at home and do your own taste test to see which your family likes better.

At Home with the Plant-Based Family

T. COLIN CAMPBELL

Author of *The China Study*, T. Colin Campbell has done extensive research behind eating plant-based. But his relationship with eating plant-based doesn't just end with research. He long ago implemented a change in diet in his own life, for himself and his family. His wife, Karen, is an enthusiastic participant, coming up with delicious recipes that their five children and ten grandchildren all enjoy.

However, eating completely plant-based didn't happen overnight. "From 1980, we ate more tuna salad and chicken salad, dropped red meat for alternative meat, then we sustained with chicken for a little while until we finally dropped that, then dropped the dairy," Colin says. During the slow progression, Karen revised traditional recipes over and over again so that they could replace the foods being dropped.

Their personal experiences with loss (Karen lost her mother to colon cancer and Colin his father from a heart attack) gave them the motivation to become even more dedicated to their change in diet. But they didn't commit 100 percent until Karen was diagnosed with advanced melanoma and Colin suffered medical issues due to his history isolating a very toxic compound in his research. Both medical issues have since been resolved, and Colin and Karen haven't looked back.

Today, all his children and grandchildren, now in college, are dedicated to the diet. His daughter LeAnne and daughter-in-law Kim have both written plant-based cookbooks: *The China Study Cookbook, The PlantPure Nation Cookbook,* and *The PlantPure Kitchen.* (LeAnne is, of course, also the editor of this book and the rest of the China Study cookbook line. You can read her profile on page 215.) And Karen still likes to experiment with recipes and try them out on Colin. "One of my favorites is mashed potatoes and kale, or beans and kale," he says. "Maybe rice; there's a Mexican one that Karen does."

With the whole family on the bandwagon, encouraging and supporting each other to stay consistently plant-based, Colin will hopefully be with us for many years to come.

SANDWICHES

GREEK HUMMUS PITAS

Hummus is a great way to get beans into the mouths of kids who might not otherwise be fans of the uber-healthy legume. My mom used to take us to a small tavern in downtown Columbus where the owner was Greek and made amazing food. My brother and I would sit at the bar and snack on his version of the yummy spread.

Makes 8 sandwiches

4 cups cooked or canned chickpeas, warmed (see Tip)

⅓ cup pine nuts, toasted and ground in a food processor or spice mill

6 garlic cloves, peeled

3 tablespoons fresh lemon juice

3 tablespoons nutritional yeast

2 teaspoons dried basil or 2 tablespoons minced fresh basil

1 teaspoon dried oregano

1 teaspoon sea salt

2 large tomatoes, sliced

2 cups mixed greens

8 whole-grain pitas, cut in half and split

1. Combine the chickpeas, pine nuts, garlic, lemon juice, nutritional yeast, basil, oregano, and sea salt in a food processor and puree until smooth and creamy. Scrape down the bowl as needed to get everything incorporated.
2. To make the sandwiches, put a tomato slice and some mixed greens in each pita half and spoon some of the hummus in with it.

 RECIPE TIP

Warmed chickpeas will give you a creamier hummus than cold chickpeas. If you are cooking your beans from scratch, make sure they are very tender before making them into hummus, and be patient when pureeing. Otherwise, the final texture will be gritty.

ODE TO PIMENTO SPREAD SANDWICHES

Your kids will love this dairy-free version of the famous spread on crackers, as a sandwich with sprouts and mixed greens, or as a dip for fresh vegetables.

Makes 6 sandwiches

1 (1-pound) package extra-firm tofu or 2 cups cooked or canned white beans

6 tablespoons almond butter

4 tablespoons miso

2 roasted red bell peppers

3 garlic cloves, peeled

2 tablespoons chopped fresh dill

12 slices whole-grain bread

3 cups mixed greens

6 ounces fresh sprouts

1. Combine the tofu, almond butter, miso, roasted bell peppers, garlic, and dill in a food processor and blend until smooth and creamy, 3 to 4 minutes. Scrape down the bowl as needed to get everything incorporated.
2. To make the sandwiches, top 6 slices of bread with some of the mixed greens. Scoop ½ cup of the pimento spread over the mixed greens, then top with some sprouts and the remaining 6 slices of bread.

📝 NOTE FOR THE COOK

Miso (fermented soybean paste) is used extensively in Asian cooking to add flavor. It is a very salty condiment, and a little goes a long way.

📝 NOTE FOR THE COOK

You can buy roasted red peppers in a jar, or you can roast your own. Carefully hold a red bell pepper over an open flame and let it char all over. Transfer it to a paper or plastic bag to steam, then peel off the blackened part by hand. Do not rinse it or you will lose all the flavor of roasting.

GRILLED CHEESE SANDWICHES

I loved grilled cheese sandwiches growing up—what kid doesn't? These days you see all kinds of gourmet grilled cheese sandwiches, but none of them can be as interesting as this recipe, because it is made without cheese and without butter!

Serves 6 to 8

1 recipe Cheese Sauce (page 98), heated
12–16 slices whole-grain bread

Heat a griddle or nonstick skillet over medium heat. Spoon some cheese sauce onto a slice of bread, top with another slice, and place the sandwich on the griddle. Toast until the bottom is golden, 3 to 4 minutes, then turn and toast the other side. Repeat for the remaining sandwiches.

📝 NOTE FOR THE COOK

The secret to toasting bread on an oil-free surface is not to leave it alone for too long. It will go from toasted to burned in the blink of an eye.

"FRIED BOLOGNA" SANDWICHES

I had a babysitter who made fried bologna sandwiches for me and my brother, and we fell in love with them. For many years I tried to replicate the flavor using commercial vegan bologna, but I knew that was not the healthiest choice. Then one day I made a grilled portobello sandwich and realized how much it tasted like my old favorite. While these mushroom slices may not look like bologna, the marinade gives them a flavor much like the original deli slices.

Makes 4 sandwiches

2 cups water

¼ cup tamari

1 tablespoon red wine vinegar

4 garlic cloves, minced

1 teaspoon granulated onion

1 teaspoon mustard powder

1 teaspoon ground coriander

½ teaspoon ground mace

½ teaspoon smoked paprika

¼ teaspoon black pepper

4 large portobello mushrooms, stems removed, caps cut in half

Mayonnaise (page 97)

8 slices whole-grain bread

Tomato slices

Lettuce leaves

1. In a shallow dish or baking pan, whisk together the water, tamari, red wine vinegar, garlic, granulated onion, mustard powder, coriander, mace, paprika, and black pepper. Add the mushrooms and marinate for at least 1 hour, or overnight in the refrigerator.

2. Heat a large nonstick skillet over medium heat for 2 minutes. Remove the mushrooms from the marinade and cook until browned on the bottom, about 4 minutes. Turn the mushrooms over and cook until they have softened and browned on the other side, another 4 minutes or so.

3. To assemble each sandwich, spread some mayonnaise on a slice of bread and top with 2 mushroom halves, a large slice of tomato, and a lettuce leaf. Cover with a second slice of bread and serve.

MLTS

My number one favorite sandwich from my childhood was the BLT. This vegan version is just as delicious and makes for a quick and easy meal the whole family will enjoy.

Makes 4 sandwiches

8 slices whole-grain bread, toasted

½ cup Mayonnaise (page 97)

1 recipe Mushroom "Bacon" (page 122)

1 large tomato, thinly sliced

4 large romaine lettuce leaves

Place 4 slices of toast on a work surface and top each with some of the mayonnaise, mushroom bacon, tomato slices, and finally, a lettuce leaf. Top with the remaining 4 slices of toast and serve.

CARROT DOGS

Kids of all ages love hot dogs—the epitome of American food. Keep these carrot dogs on hand so your kids can have them whenever they want a quick meal. I like mine with Lentil Chili (page 179), but let your kids choose their favorite toppings.

Makes 6 sandwiches

6 large carrots, peeled and trimmed to fit your hot dog buns

2 cups water

¼ cup tamari

1 tablespoon red wine vinegar

4 garlic cloves, minced

1 teaspoon granulated onion

1 teaspoon mustard powder

1 teaspoon ground coriander

½ teaspoon ground mace

½ teaspoon smoked paprika

¼ teaspoon black pepper

6 hot dog buns, toasted if desired

1. Bring a 2-quart pot of water to a boil over medium-high heat. Add the carrots and bring the water back to a boil. Reduce the heat to medium and let the carrots cook until they are tender, 8 to 10 minutes. Drain the carrots and rinse them under cool water to stop the cooking.
2. While the carrots are cooking, whisk together the water, tamari, red wine vinegar, garlic, granulated onion, mustard powder, coriander, mace, smoked paprika, and black pepper in a baking dish. Add the carrots to the marinade and toss to coat. Cover the dish and refrigerate for at least 12 hours.
3. Heat a large skillet over medium-high heat. Add the carrots and the marinade and cook, turning the carrots occasionally, until most of the marinade has evaporated and the carrots have started to brown, about 10 minutes.
4. Serve in a bun with your favorite toppings.

🍲 **RECIPE TIP**

Be sure to choose carrots of equal size so they all cook in the same amount of time.

SLOPPY JOES

Sloppy Joes are another of my favorite childhood sandwiches. We ate them on white bread and Mom always made the filling from scratch, never from a can. This version, made with high-fiber, vitamin- and mineral-rich wheat berries, has all of the flavor that kids love in a Sloppy Joe without the unwanted animal protein or fat.

Makes 6 sandwiches

1 medium yellow onion, finely chopped

½ green bell pepper, finely chopped

1 celery stalk, finely chopped

2 garlic cloves, minced

2 cups cooked wheat berries (see Tip)

1 (15-ounce) can tomato puree

⅓ cup Date Puree (page 241)

¼ cup ketchup

1 tablespoon vegan Worcestershire sauce or tamari

Sea salt and black pepper

6 whole-grain hamburger buns

1. Sauté the onion, bell pepper, and celery in a medium-size skillet over medium heat for 7 to 8 minutes. Add water 1 to 2 tablespoons at a time to keep the vegetables from sticking to the pan. Add the garlic and cook for another minute.
2. Add the cooked wheat berries, tomato puree, date puree, ketchup, and Worcestershire sauce, and cook, stirring occasionally, until the sauce thickens, about 10 minutes. Season with sea salt and black pepper to taste.
3. Place the bottom halves of each hamburger bun on a work surface and top with some of the filling. Place the tops of the buns on the sandwiches and serve.

🛎 RECIPE TIP

Wheat berries can be found at natural food stores and online retailers. To cook them, combine ⅔ cup wheat berries and 2 cups water in a small saucepan. Bring the water to a boil over medium-high heat, reduce the heat to medium, cover, and cook for 50 to 60 minutes, until the water is absorbed and the wheat berries are tender.

PORTOBELLO REUBENS

Reubens somehow seem to me a grown-up sandwich, but I have been eating them since I was a teenager. See whether your kids have a "grown-up palate" with this plant-based version.

Makes 4 sandwiches

4 large portobello mushroom caps

2 cups water

¼ cup low-sodium tamari

1 tablespoon red wine vinegar

4 garlic cloves, minced

1 teaspoon mustard powder

1 teaspoon granulated onion

1 teaspoon ground coriander

¼ teaspoon ground cloves

¼ teaspoon ground ginger

¼ teaspoon black pepper

8 slices whole-grain rye bread, toasted

¾ cup Thousand Island Dressing (page 119)

1½ cups sauerkraut, drained

1 cup Cheese Sauce (page 98)

1. Place the mushrooms in a single layer in a shallow baking dish.
2. In a small bowl, whisk together the water, tamari, red wine vinegar, garlic, mustard powder, granulated onion, coriander, cloves, ginger, and black pepper. Pour the mixture over the mushrooms and let sit for 30 minutes. Turn the mushrooms over and let sit for another 30 minutes.
3. Heat a large nonstick skillet over medium heat for 2 minutes. Place the mushrooms in the pan and cook for 2 minutes. Turn them over, drizzle about ½ cup of the marinade over the mushrooms, and let them cook until the marinade is mostly evaporated.

4. Place 4 slices of rye toast on a work surface. Place a mushroom on each and top each with some of the dressing and sauerkraut. Spread some of the cheese sauce on the 4 remaining slices of rye toast and place on top of the sandwiches. Serve.

 RECIPE TIP

If you (or your kids) are not fans of mushrooms, try replacing them in this dish with eggplant or zucchini slices.

MEDITERRANEAN MELTS

Kids in my cooking classes love these sandwiches, much to the surprise of some parents, who say their kids would never eat a sandwich like this at home. It just goes to show you that kids are sometimes more sophisticated than we think they are.

Makes 4 sandwiches

8 slices whole-grain bread
1 recipe Cheese Sauce (page 98)
1 recipe Meatballs (page 199), crumbled

1. Place 4 slices of bread on a work surface and spread ¼ cup of the sauce over each. Spoon some of the crumbled meatballs over the sauce. Spoon on another ¼ cup of the sauce. Top with the remaining bread slices.
2. Heat a large nonstick skillet or griddle over medium heat. Place the sandwiches in the heated skillet and toast until lightly browned on the bottom, about 2 minutes. Gently turn the sandwiches over and toast the other side until the bread is lightly browned, another 2 minutes or so. Serve.

📝 NOTE FOR THE COOK

The secret to toasting bread on an oil-free surface is not to leave it alone for too long. It will go from toasted to burned in the blink of an eye.

MEDITERRANEAN "MEATBALL" SUBS

My friend Jenny makes meatball subs for her kids every Friday night. One night when I was babysitting the kids, they begged for their favorite Friday night treat. I made them this version, complete with Green Goddess Slaw. Now they ask their mom to make it my way!

Makes 6 subs

6 whole-grain sub buns
1 (28-ounce) jar spaghetti sauce
1 recipe Meatballs (page 199)
1 recipe Cheese Sauce (page 98)
1 recipe Green Goddess Slaw (page 125)

1. Preheat the oven to 375°F.
2. Split open the sub buns and line them up on a baking sheet.
3. Spread ½ cup spaghetti sauce on the bottom half of each bun, then place 3 meatballs on top of the sauce. Pour another ½ cup spaghetti sauce over the meatballs, then pour ⅓ cup cheese sauce over the meatballs. Bake until the cheese sauce is bubbly and the bread is toasted, 12 to 14 minutes.
4. Top with the slaw and fold the top half of the bun over the filling to serve.

At Home with the Plant-Based Family

BEVERLY GRANDISON

Some people decide to follow a plant-based diet because they simply want a change, because they feel they are lacking energy, or because they want to improve their overall health for themselves and their families. For Beverly Grandison, the decision to become plant-based involved much more. Thirteen years ago, she was working as a military officer in the army, carrying on a completely normal, active lifestyle (which included jumping out of planes). When chronic fatigue set in, she knew something wasn't right. In January of 2005, after she'd undergone tests for almost two years to determine the cause of her illness, half of Beverly's face went numb, most of her sense of taste disappeared, and she couldn't lift anything with her right hand. After a barrage of more tests, she was eventually diagnosed with multiple sclerosis. That diagnosis was life altering for Beverly, as she really enjoyed the military and it was her life.

With no history of the disease in her family, Beverly found herself faced with a lot of questions, few answers, and an onslaught of prescriptions for multiple medications. At one point, doctors approached Beverly about inserting a plate and screw in her neck in order to help the numbing and lack of mobility that was setting in. However, instead of filling those prescriptions and having the recommended surgery, she chose to follow a holistic approach to treating her disease. With her husband, Johnny, who had been diagnosed with Crohn's disease, Beverly turned to a whole food, plant-based diet and immediately noticed changes. Beverly opted out of the surgery and, after her change in diet, regained almost all of her original mobility.

"Today, I can turn my head left, right, up, down, put my earrings on, and button my buttons. Although there is still disc damage from jumping out of planes, by improving my diet to plant-based, I've been able to reverse and slow down a lot of the degeneration that was happening and live a better quality of life." Even her husband made medical strides. His Crohn's disease is in remission thanks to plant-based eating.

What started as a medical crisis turned into a journey of self-discovery that helped her and her husband improve their quality of health long term. "I saw a picture of us from six years ago and I look better today than I did then . . . It's just a matter over these years of being consistent, deliberate, intentional, and faithful to what I believe in," Beverly says. "I tell people, I live in freedom, no medications, I wake up with energy, I go to bed with energy." Johnny is a happy man as well.

While her husband has been part of the dietary change from the beginning, the rest of Beverly's family and in-laws haven't understood their new diet and lifestyle. Even coming from a family of mixed diets (her youngest sister and father are vegan; her other sister has recently become vegetarian, and her brothers eat a standard American diet), Beverly knows that staying on the path isn't always easy. She grew up in a West Indian/Caribbean home in Florida and her husband, Johnny, grew up in Alabama, where meat was a staple of every meal. Beverly says, "Although my family incorporated fruits and vegetables into our diet, we didn't have an understanding of how vital they are to good health."

With this kind of culinary history, some of her family and friends were understandably resistant to hearing about a plant-based diet and at first this caused some tension. Even Beverly had doubts in the beginning when her sister told her to stop drinking milk after her diagnosis. She told her sister, "I grew up on whole milk and I'll die drinking whole milk." Her sister's comment back was, "Yep, you'll die prematurely . . ."

"As I matured and learned more about the direct link between disease and nutrition, I realized all I could do is supply knowledge and information and they have to figure this out themselves, in their time, and hopefully not too late," Beverly says.

In fact, the more her family and friends see the differences a plant-based diet has made in her own life, the more they come to Beverly for advice on the subject of health. "They see my life, and they see what I look like. I no longer try to convince or persuade my family and close friends; I don't bother them anymore. Now they're coming to me." Instead of trying to force friends and family to change, Beverly took a step back, waiting in the wings to support their transitions whenever they are ready.

Perhaps the most enthusiastic member of her family is her husband, Johnny. "He definitely likes my bean dish. I call it a bean taco casserole, a recipe I transformed from a previously very unhealthy one!" Even though Johnny is "probably 80 percent plant-based," he is 100 percent supportive of Beverly. Although the road was rocky, Beverly can't thank God, education, and the whole foods, plant-based lifestyle enough.

"I can't put a price tag on what I've learned and what it has done for my health, and the health of my family, friends, and clients. We are inspiring healthy living and impacting generations to come."

SOUPS

CREAM OF TOMATO SOUP

When I was a kid, we almost always had cream of tomato soup with grilled cheese sandwiches. This is my healthy version of that popular canned soup. Try it with my favorite Grilled Cheese Sandwiches (page 145).

Serves 6 to 8

1 medium yellow onion, diced

4 garlic cloves, minced

4 cups low-sodium vegetable broth

1 (28-ounce) can diced tomatoes, undrained

1 (12-ounce) bag frozen cauliflower or 2 cups fresh cauliflower florets

4 pitted dates (optional)

1 cup fresh basil leaves, shredded

Sea salt and black pepper

1. Sauté the onion in a large saucepan over medium heat until the onion turns translucent and starts to brown, about 8 minutes. Add water 1 to 2 tablespoons at a time to keep the onion from sticking. Add the garlic and cook for another minute.
2. Add the vegetable broth, diced tomatoes, cauliflower, and dates (if using); cover; and cook for 15 minutes. Add the basil, season with sea salt and black pepper to taste, and cook for another 5 minutes to marry the flavors.
3. Puree the soup in batches in a blender or use an immersion blender to puree the soup right in the pot. Taste and adjust for salt and serve.

📝 NOTE FOR THE COOK

When pureeing hot liquids in a countertop blender, remove the center of the blender lid and hold a dish towel firmly over the hole to catch the released steam. Start the blender on low and slowly increase the speed.

SWEET POTATO BISQUE

I have loved creamy soups since I was a kid. My first such soup was Campbell's Cream of Tomato, and it was many years before I had a creamy soup that didn't come from a can. This bisque was one of the first, and in addition to being much healthier than any canned soup I ever ate as a kid, it tastes great.

Serves 6

1 medium yellow onion, chopped

2 garlic cloves, minced

1 tablespoon minced fresh ginger

1½ teaspoons ground cinnamon

Pinch ground allspice

Grated zest and juice of 1 orange

1 (14.5-ounce) can diced tomatoes, undrained

2 pounds sweet potatoes, peeled and chopped (about 4 medium)

4 cups low-sodium vegetable broth

¼ cup creamy cashew butter

Sea salt and black pepper

Unsweetened plant milk, as needed

Sliced scallions, for garnish

1. Sauté the onion in a large saucepan over medium heat until it turns translucent and starts to brown, about 8 minutes. Add water 1 to 2 tablespoons at a time to keep the onion from sticking. Add the garlic, ginger, cinnamon, and allspice, and cook for another minute.
2. Add the orange zest and juice, tomatoes, sweet potatoes, and vegetable broth. Cover and cook until the sweet potatoes are tender, about 20 minutes.
3. Add the cashew butter to the pan, season the soup with sea salt and black pepper to taste, and cook for another minute.
4. Puree the soup in batches in a blender or use an immersion blender to puree the soup right in the pot. Add plant milk as needed to make the soup as creamy as you wish. Serve, garnished with scallions.

📝 NOTE FOR THE COOK

The key to cutting potatoes safely is carefully cutting them in half so that they sit with stability on the work surface, and then cutting each half as you wish.

📝 NOTE FOR THE COOK

When pureeing hot liquids in a countertop blender, remove the center of the blender lid and hold a dish towel firmly over the hole to catch the released steam. Start the blender on low and slowly increase the speed.

POTATO SOUP

Feel free to omit the mushrooms in this recipe; some kids like mushrooms, but for others it's an acquired taste. Either way, serve this delicious soup on its own or with bread for dipping.

Serves 6 to 8

1 large yellow onion, diced

2 large carrots, peeled and diced

3 celery stalks, diced

8 ounces button mushrooms, sliced (optional)

6 cups low-sodium vegetable broth

2 pounds russet potatoes, peeled and diced

1 tablespoon minced fresh dill, plus more for garnish

1 tablespoon dried basil (if using mushrooms)

1 teaspoon dried thyme

2 cups Cheese Sauce (page 98), or 2 cups unsweetened plant milk mixed with 2 tablespoons arrowroot powder

Sea salt and black pepper

1. Sauté the onion, carrots, celery, and mushrooms (if using) in a large saucepan over medium heat until the onion turns translucent and starts to brown, about 8 minutes. Add water 1 to 2 tablespoons at a time to keep the vegetables from sticking.

2. Add the vegetable broth, potatoes, dill, basil, and thyme. Cover and cook until the potatoes are tender, about 20 minutes.

3. Add the cheese sauce, season with sea salt and black pepper to taste, and cook another for 5 minutes.

4. To serve, ladle the soup into bowls and garnish each serving with additional fresh dill.

📝 NOTE FOR THE COOK

The key to cutting potatoes safely is carefully cutting them in half so that they sit with stability on the work surface, and then cutting each half as you wish.

POTATO, CABBAGE, AND WHITE BEAN SOUP

My mom used to make a version of this soup that was full of vegetables, but often also had some kind of meat in it. This version, made with beans, is much healthier for kids and grown-ups alike and is still just as tasty as my mom's. Just don't tell her I said that!

Serves 8

1 large yellow onion, diced

3 celery stalks, diced

3 large carrots, peeled and diced

6 garlic cloves, minced

6 cups chopped green cabbage

2 large russet potatoes, peeled and diced (see Note on page 54)

3 (15-ounce) cans white beans, rinsed and drained, or 4½ cups cooked white beans (see Tip)

8 cups low-sodium vegetable broth

3 tablespoons chopped fresh dill

Grated zest of 1 lemon

Sea salt and black pepper

1. Sauté the onion, celery, and carrots in a large saucepan over medium heat until the onion turns translucent and starts to brown, about 8 minutes. Add water 1 to 2 tablespoons at a time to keep the vegetables from sticking. Add the garlic and cook for another minute.

2. Add the cabbage, potatoes, beans, vegetable broth, and dill. Turn the heat up to high and bring the liquid to a boil. Reduce the heat to medium and simmer the soup until the potatoes are tender and the soup has thickened, about 15 minutes.

3. Add the lemon zest, season with sea salt and black pepper to taste, and cook for another 5 minutes. Serve.

 **RECIPE TIP**

Any white beans will work in this recipe—Great Northern, cannellini, or navy—so use whatever you have on hand.

SWEET POTATO, SWISS CHARD, AND RED LENTIL SOUP

The only time we ate sweet potatoes as kids was during the holidays in a casserole topped with marshmallows. Now I eat them any way I can get them and love them in soups for the earthy sweetness they add.

Serves 6

1 large yellow onion, diced

2 celery stalks, diced

2 large carrots, peeled and diced

4 garlic cloves, minced

1 tablespoon ground cumin

¼ teaspoon ground allspice

1 large sweet potato, peeled and diced

2 cups red lentils

4 cups low-sodium vegetable broth, plus more as needed

1 large bunch Swiss chard, chopped

Sea salt and black pepper

Juice of 1 lemon

---

1. Sauté the onion, celery, and carrots in a large saucepan over medium heat until the onion turns translucent and starts to brown, about 8 minutes. Add water 1 to 2 tablespoons at a time to keep the vegetables from sticking. Add the garlic, cumin, and allspice and cook for another minute.
2. Add the sweet potato, lentils, and vegetable broth. Turn the heat up to high and bring the liquid to a boil. Reduce the heat to medium and simmer the soup until the sweet potatoes and lentils are tender, about 20 minutes.
3. Add the chard, season with sea salt and black pepper to taste, and simmer until the chard is cooked, about 10 minutes. Stir in the lemon juice and serve.

📝 NOTE FOR THE COOK

The key to cutting potatoes safely is carefully cutting them in half so that they sit with stability on the work surface, and then cutting each half as you wish.

🍽 RECIPE TIP

Swiss chard is a mild green with a spinach-like flavor. If you can't find Swiss chard or its relative rainbow chard, you can use spinach. Spinach cooks more quickly than chard, so it needs only about 5 minutes to cook once it's added to the soup.

BLACK-EYED PEA GUMBO

Ham, shrimp, and sausage are traditional ingredients in gumbo, but this plant-based version is every bit as hearty and delicious—and a lot healthier. I like to serve gumbo the way my dad did, with cornbread alongside. Try this with Sweet Potato Cornbread (page 85).

Serves 6 to 8

½ cup whole wheat pastry flour

1 medium yellow onion, chopped

1 medium green bell pepper, seeded and chopped

5 celery stalks, chopped

4 garlic cloves, minced

2 teaspoons dried thyme

2 large tomatoes, diced

4 cups cooked brown rice (page 106)

4 (15-ounce) cans black-eyed peas, drained, or 6 cups cooked black-eyed peas

2 cups low-sodium vegetable broth

Sea salt and black pepper

1. Sprinkle the flour in a small skillet and toast it over medium-low heat until it starts to turn brown and fragrant. Set it aside while you finish the rest of the dish.

2. Sauté the onion, bell pepper, and celery in a large saucepan over medium heat until the onion turns translucent and starts to brown, about 8 minutes. Add water 1 to 2 tablespoons at a time to keep the vegetables from sticking. Add the garlic and thyme and cook for another minute.

3. Add the toasted flour, diced tomatoes, rice, black-eyed peas, and vegetable broth. Turn the heat up to high and bring the liquid to a boil. Reduce the heat to low and simmer until the soup is thick and a rich gravy has formed, about 45 minutes. Season with sea salt and black pepper and cook for another 5 minutes. Serve.

 **RECIPE TIP**

In traditional gumbos, flour is cooked with some fat, often butter, to toast it. Even if you're just dry-toasting the flour as in this version, remember that the browner the flour, the more flavor it gives to the final dish.

LENTIL CHILI

Cincinnati-style chili adds just a touch of sweetness with spices like cinnamon or allspice. This healthy version made with lentils is full of fiber, without the unwanted animal ingredients.

Serves 4

1 medium yellow onion, diced

4 garlic cloves, minced

2 tablespoons ancho chile powder

1 tablespoon ground cumin

½ teaspoon ground cinnamon

Pinch ground cloves (see Note)

4 cups water

2 cups green lentils

1 (15-ounce) can tomato puree

Sea salt and black pepper

1. Sauté the onion in a large saucepan over medium heat until it turns translucent and starts to brown, about 8 minutes. Add water 1 to 2 tablespoons at a time to keep the onion from sticking. Add the garlic, chile powder, cumin, cinnamon, and cloves, and cook for another minute.

2. Add the water and lentils, cover, and cook until the lentils are tender, about 45 minutes.

3. Add the tomato puree, season with sea salt and black pepper to taste, and cook until the sauce is bubbly and thickens a little, about 10 minutes. Serve.

📝 NOTE FOR THE COOK

Be careful when measuring spices like ground cloves, because a little goes a long way. A pinch of cloves is equal to about 1/16 teaspoon.

WHITE BEAN AND SQUASH CHILI

Chili can be adapted in countless ways to suit your preference for ingredients, flavor, spiciness, and texture. When I started cooking for myself at the age of eleven, I got to choose what I made and how I made it. Score one for learning how to cook at an early age!

Serves 8

2 tablespoons ancho chile powder

1 large yellow onion, chopped

2 red bell peppers, seeded and chopped

4 garlic cloves, minced

1 tablespoon ground cumin, toasted (see Note)

1 medium butternut squash, peeled, seeded, and diced

4 (15-ounce) cans white beans, rinsed and drained, or 6 cups cooked white beans (see Tip)

5 cups low-sodium vegetable broth

Sea salt and black pepper

1. Sprinkle the ancho chile powder in a small skillet and toast it over low heat until it starts to turn brown and fragrant. Set it aside while you finish the rest of the dish.

2. Sauté the onion in a large saucepan over medium heat until it turns translucent and starts to brown, about 8 minutes. Add water 1 to 2 tablespoons at a time to keep the onion from sticking.

3. Add the bell pepper and cook for another 5 minutes. Add the garlic, cumin, and toasted ancho chile powder, and cook for another minute.

4. Add the squash, beans, and vegetable broth; cover; and cook until the squash is tender, 10 to 12 minutes.

5. Season with sea salt and black pepper to taste, cook for another 10 minutes, and serve.

 ## NOTE FOR THE COOK

Toasting spices is tricky because they go from fragrant to burned in a split second. You can't walk away from the stove for even a minute.

 ## RECIPE TIP

Any white beans will work in this recipe—Great Northern, cannellini, or navy—so use whatever you have on hand.

At Home with the Plant-Based Family

GARRETT COLBURN

I first met Garrett Colburn when he worked as an intern at Wellness Forum Health. He had learned from his sister and mother about the plant-based diet and wanted to explore how to cook different kinds of plant-based recipes for himself and his family. Garrett comes from what I like to call a blended family: a family where some members eat plant-based and some do not.

Garrett's sister, Jessie, was the initial plant-based eater in the family. She was attending Miami University, taking a general education science course in which she watched *Food, Inc.* This experience prompted her to give up meat. She then eventually gave up dairy and eggs in order to help her sensitive digestive system, per her doctor's suggestion. She felt the difference almost immediately.

His mother, Amy, who'd given up hot dogs and hamburgers long before, "started by really kind of supporting Jessie in that," she says. "It was easy for me to give up meat and then Garrett and I both did. It was just a slow progression to what we stopped eating." Initially, Garrett was resistant to changing diets, but after reading *The China Study*, he decided he wanted to try it out.

"When I was transitioning, I felt better, but then when I went whole foods, plant-based, it was pretty immediate that I felt a lot better.

Energy-wise, I wasn't tired, I didn't have this oily, gross feeling about me that I always had growing up." A dedicated athlete, he noticed the change in diminishing recovery time when working out. Rather than completing one workout for the day, he is now able to do multiple activities in the day, all with the same energy.

Amy had a different transition experience. When she was in the early stages, she began "eating a lot of processed food and a lot of bread and a lot of pasta. I really wasn't increasing my fruits and vegetables very much. I did not feel any better; I felt horrible," she says. "I thought I had no energy, I was tired." She even began gaining weight on the plant-based diet because it was also a high-carb diet. What finally allowed her to not only lose weight but also keep it off? Expanding her cooking repertoire to incorporate more whole foods and more varied plants!

One of the biggest myths around plant-based eating is the protein myth: the idea that you do not get enough protein on this diet to be healthy. But as Garrett says, "I'm still able to gain lean muscle, recover quickly, and not need this absurd amount of protein. I get a very adequate amount from just plants—rice, broccoli, and spinach are pretty high in it."

While Garrett, Jessie, and Amy are all on board for the long haul, they haven't yet convinced Garrett and Jessie's father to transition to a plant-based diet. He does enjoy some of the food that Garrett prepares, but when they eat meals together, he often also grills some meat or adds a sandwich.

When it comes to convincing more reticent members of blended families, Garrett says, "I think my advice is that everyone has to make their own decision and that showing is better than telling. Because I know how stubborn I am, I know how stubborn my dad is and my sister is." The Colburn family has seen how powerful leading by example can be.

ENTRÉES

QUESADILLAS

Quesadillas are simply corn or wheat tortillas filled with cheese and sometimes vegetables. If you keep Cheese Sauce (page 98) on hand and salsa in the fridge, you can serve this easy meal to your family in minutes—or let them make it for themselves.

Serves 6

1 large yellow onion, thinly sliced

1 large green bell pepper, seeded and thinly sliced

8 ounces button mushrooms, sliced

Sea salt and black pepper

1 recipe Cheese Sauce (page 98)

6 large whole-grain tortillas

Favorite salsa

1 recipe Sour Cream (page 94)

1. Sauté the onion, bell pepper, and mushrooms in a large saucepan over medium heat until the onion turns translucent and starts to brown, about 8 minutes. Add water 1 to 2 tablespoons at a time to keep the vegetables from sticking.

2. Season the vegetables with sea salt and black pepper to taste. Stir in the cheese sauce and cook until heated through. Set aside.

3. Heat a large skillet over medium heat for 1 minute. Place a tortilla on your work surface and spoon on one-third of the vegetable mixture, then place another tortilla on top of it. Transfer the quesadilla to the skillet and heat until lightly browned, about 2 minutes. Carefully turn the quesadilla over and brown the other side. Repeat with the remaining tortillas and vegetables.

4. To serve, cut each quesadilla into 6 wedges and serve with the salsa and sour cream.

CORN AND MASHED POTATO CAKES

This recipe is an easy way to use up leftover mashed potatoes—and delicious, too! My mom used to fry them, but my baked version is just as good, without all the fat.

Serves 6

2 pounds russet potatoes, scrubbed and diced

1 (12-ounce) bag frozen corn, thawed, or 2 cups fresh corn

1 medium yellow onion, diced

1 medium red bell pepper, seeded and diced

⅓ cup whole wheat pastry flour, plus more for dusting the cakes

½ teaspoon sea salt

½ teaspoon ground black pepper

1 recipe Sour Cream (page 94)

1. Preheat the oven to 350°F.
2. Put the potatoes in a pot and cover with cold water. Bring the water to a boil over high heat, reduce the heat to medium, and simmer the potatoes until tender, 10 to 12 minutes. Drain the potatoes, reserving 1½ cups of the cooking liquid.
3. Return the potatoes to the pot and mash them, adding enough of the reserved cooking liquid to keep them from being gummy.
4. In a large bowl, combine the mashed potatoes, corn, onion, bell pepper, flour, sea salt, and black pepper. Put some additional flour in a shallow dish.
5. Using a large ice cream scoop, form the potato mixture into balls, coat them lightly in the extra flour, and place them on a nonstick baking sheet or a regular baking sheet lined with parchment paper. Flatten each ball into a ½-inch-thick patty.
6. Bake the potato cakes until the edges start to brown, about 20 minutes, then turn them over and bake for another 15 minutes.
7. Serve warm, with the sour cream.

CHILAQUILES FRITTATA

Chilaquiles is a popular Mexican dish in which corn tortillas are cooked with salsa and eggs or refried beans. Here the dish is prepared frittata style—like an open-face omelet. If your Spanish language skills are any good, you can teach your kids how to pronounce fun words like this one. If not, maybe they can give you a pronunciation lesson.

Serves 4

1 large yellow onion, chopped

4 garlic cloves, minced

1 teaspoon ground cumin

1 recipe Corn Chips (page 86)

1 (15-ounce) can black beans, rinsed and drained, or 1½ cups cooked black beans

Sea salt and black pepper

1 (12-ounce) package extra-firm silken tofu

¼ cup chickpea flour

2 tablespoons nutritional yeast

1 cup favorite enchilada sauce or salsa

1 cup Queso Sauce (page 100)

1 cup chopped scallion, for garnish

1 cup chopped fresh cilantro, for garnish

1. Preheat the oven to 350°F.
2. In a large nonstick skillet, sauté the onion over medium heat until it turns translucent and starts to brown, about 8 minutes. Add water 1 to 2 tablespoons at a time to keep the onion from sticking. Add the garlic and cumin and cook for another minute.
3. Add the corn chips and black beans, season with sea salt and black pepper to taste, and remove the pan from the heat.
4. In a food processor, combine the silken tofu, chickpea flour, nutritional yeast, ¾ teaspoon sea salt, and black pepper to taste. Puree until smooth and creamy.
5. Transfer the tofu mixture to the pan with the black bean mixture and mix well. Pour the mixture into a nonstick 9-inch pie pan or nonstick 8-inch square baking dish. Bake for 30 minutes.
6. Turn the broiler on high. Top the frittata with the enchilada sauce and then drizzle the queso sauce over the enchilada sauce. Broil until the queso sauce is lightly browned, 7 to 8 minutes.
7. Allow the frittata to stand for 10 minutes before cutting. Serve garnished with the chopped scallion and cilantro.

🍲 RECIPE TIP

A nonstick skillet is essential for a dish like this. Be sure to use wooden or plastic utensils when using a nonstick skillet so you don't scrape off the finish.

🍲 RECIPE TIP

Many recipes in this book call for your choice of silken tofu or canned white beans. This is one recipe where beans don't make a good substitute for the tofu.

THAI-STYLE PEANUT NOODLES

This simple Thai dish is full of flavor, and kids love it. If you keep the peanut sauce on hand, the dish comes together very quickly.

Serves 4

PEANUT SAUCE

⅓ cup smooth peanut butter

¼ cup pure maple syrup

3 tablespoons low-sodium tamari

1½ tablespoons rice vinegar

1 teaspoon minced fresh ginger

2 garlic cloves, minced

Water, as needed

VEGETABLES AND NOODLES

12 ounces whole-grain noodles

1 small yellow onion, cut into thin slivers

1 large tomato, chopped

1 cup chopped fresh basil

1 cup chopped fresh cilantro

Toasted peanuts (see Note on page 43), for garnish

1. To make the peanut sauce, in a small bowl whisk together the peanut butter, maple syrup, tamari, rice vinegar, ginger, and garlic. Thin the sauce with a little water if needed to achieve a creamy consistency. Set aside.
2. To make the vegetables and noodles, cook the whole-grain noodles according to the package instructions. Drain and set aside.
3. While the noodles cook, sauté the onion in a large skillet over medium-high heat until it starts to brown, about 3 minutes. Add the tomato and cook for another minute.
4. Add the peanut sauce, cooked noodles, basil, and cilantro, and cook until heated through. Serve garnished with the toasted peanuts.

THAI-STYLE NOODLES WITH CASHEWS AND PINEAPPLE

I was lucky enough to have parents who were explorers of good food and who introduced us to new foods as they discovered them. I imagine that their open-mindedness about food played a big part in my own open-mindedness. If you don't think of your kids as adventurous eaters, maybe it's because you haven't introduced them to enough interesting new foods!

Serves 4 to 6

1 pound whole-grain linguine

1 tablespoon arrowroot powder

1 cup low-sodium vegetable broth

1½ cups canned lite coconut milk

3 tablespoons tamari, or to taste

1 tablespoon Thai red curry paste

1 tablespoon curry powder

Grated zest and juice of 1 lime

2 teaspoons crushed red pepper flakes

1 medium yellow onion, thinly sliced

1 red bell pepper, seeded and cut into 1-inch squares

3 cups sliced bok choy

3 garlic cloves, minced

1½ cups coarsely chopped fresh pineapple

½ cup toasted cashews (see Note on page 43), for garnish

¼ cup finely chopped fresh basil, for garnish

¼ cup finely chopped fresh cilantro, for garnish

3 tablespoons finely chopped fresh mint, for garnish

1. Cook the whole-grain linguine according to the package instructions, then drain and rinse under cold water until cool. Set aside.
2. While the linguine is cooking, in a medium-size bowl, whisk the arrowroot powder into the vegetable broth. Whisk in the coconut milk, tamari, curry paste, curry powder, lime zest and juice, and red pepper flakes. Set aside.
3. Sauté the onion and bell pepper in a large skillet over medium-high heat until the onion turns translucent and starts to brown, about 5 minutes. Add water 1 to 2 tablespoons at a time to keep the vegetables from sticking. Add the bok choy and garlic and cook for another minute.
4. Stir in the red curry paste mixture, pineapple, and cooked linguine, and cook until heated through. Serve, garnished with the cashews and chopped fresh herbs.

RECIPE TIP

Coconut milk has a lot of fat in it and should be used sparingly. I like its flavor, but I often make this dish instead with 1½ cups unsweetened plant milk thickened with 1 tablespoon arrowroot powder and flavored with ¼ teaspoon coconut extract. Use the extract sparingly, as it can overpower the dish.

PORTOBELLO PEPPER STEAK

We kids loved anything my mom made that had a gravy, and this dish was no exception. Her version was very rich, full of saturated fat from meat and butter. This version has none of the unwanted fat, but lots of flavors kids will love.

Serves 4

⅓ cup whole wheat pastry flour

1 large yellow onion, thinly sliced

3 large bell peppers (preferably 1 red, 1 green, and 1 yellow), seeded and thinly sliced

1 pound portobello mushrooms, stems removed, caps cut into ½-inch-thick slices

6 garlic cloves, minced

1 tablespoon dried basil

2 teaspoons dried thyme

1 teaspoon dried marjoram

1 (28-ounce) can crushed tomatoes

1 cup unsweetened plant milk

1 tablespoon mellow white miso

1 tablespoon nutritional yeast

Sea salt and black pepper

4 cups cooked brown rice (page 106) or mashed potatoes

1. Sprinkle the flour in a small skillet and toast it over medium-low heat until it starts to turn brown and fragrant. Set it aside while you finish the rest of the dish.
2. Sauté the onion, bell peppers, and mushrooms in a large saucepan over medium-high heat until the onion turns translucent and starts to brown, about 8 minutes. Add water 1 to 2 tablespoons at a time to keep the vegetables from sticking. Add the garlic, basil, thyme, and marjoram, and cook for another minute.
3. Add the crushed tomatoes and reduce the heat to medium. Cover the pan and cook for 15 minutes.
4. In a blender, puree the toasted flour, plant milk, and miso. Add the mixture to the pan with the vegetables, along with the nutritional yeast. Season with sea salt and black pepper to taste and cook until a gravy develops, about 5 minutes.
5. Serve over brown rice.

📝 NOTE FOR THE COOK

Toasting flour is tricky because it goes from fragrant to burned in a split second. You can't walk away from the stove for even a minute.

🍲 RECIPE TIP

While I like the color of the three different bell peppers, when all I have is green bell peppers, I am happy to use them instead. But remember, we eat with our eyes as well as our sense of smell and our taste buds, so how a dish looks is part of how it tastes.

SPAGHETTI AND MEATBALLS

Use this master meatball recipe for anything from Swedish meatballs to barbecue-style meatballs—it all depends on what sauce you use.

Serves 6

MEATBALLS

1½ cups water

¾ cup millet

1 small yellow onion, finely diced

4 garlic cloves, minced

1 tablespoon dried basil

1 teaspoon ground fennel seed

1 teaspoon crushed red pepper flakes (optional)

¼ cup finely chopped sun-dried tomatoes

¼ cup finely chopped artichoke hearts

¼ cup coarsely ground toasted pine nuts or walnuts (see Note on page 43; optional)

1 teaspoon sea salt

SPAGHETTI

1 pound whole-grain spaghetti

1 (28-ounce) jar spaghetti sauce, heated

Chopped fresh parsley, for garnish

1. Preheat the oven to 375°F.
2. To make the meatballs, combine the water and millet in a small saucepan and bring the water to a boil over high heat. Reduce the heat to medium-low and cook the millet until it is very tender, about 20 minutes. If it is not tender after all the water is absorbed, add another 2 to 3 tablespoons of water and let it cook for another 5 minutes.
3. While the millet cooks, sauté the onion in a large skillet over medium-high heat until it turns translucent and starts to brown, about 5 minutes. Add the garlic, basil, fennel, and red pepper flakes (if using), and cook for another

minute. Add the sun-dried tomatoes, artichoke hearts, and nuts (if using), and remove the pan from the heat.

4. When the millet is done cooking, add it to the pan with the onion mixture, add the sea salt, and mix well. Shape the mixture into balls using a medium ice cream scoop or a ⅓-cup measure and place on a nonstick baking sheet.

5. Bake for 15 minutes, turn over, and continue baking until the millet balls are lightly browned, about 15 minutes more.

6. To make the spaghetti, while the meatballs are baking, cook the spaghetti according to the package instructions and drain.

7. Transfer the cooked spaghetti to a large platter. Top with the meatballs and then the spaghetti sauce. Garnish with the parsley and serve.

RECIPE TIP

Unlike traditional meatballs, these millet balls do not sit well in tomato sauce or gravy for any length of time. Be sure to add sauce to them just before serving so they don't fall apart.

NOTE FOR THE COOK

For the millet to work as a binder (to hold everything together in a patty) in this dish, you need to almost overcook it. If it seems crumbly when you first make it, add 2 to 3 tablespoons more water to the pan, cover tightly, and let it cook for another 2 to 3 minutes. The millet should hold together when pinched between your fingers or pressed against the side of the pan.

RAMEN

This is nothing like the instant ramen you might have had. This more authentic, healthy version is fun for kids because they can arrange the ingredients in the bowl themselves before adding the broth.

Serves 4

2 large leeks, light green and white parts, thinly sliced

8 cups low-sodium vegetable broth

1 large piece kombu (see Tip)

8 dried shiitake mushrooms

1 tablespoon grated fresh ginger

Low-sodium tamari (optional)

Pinch ground cloves (see Note)

1 large sweet potato, peeled and diced

Sea salt and black pepper

⅓ cup mellow white miso

8 ounces brown rice spaghetti or linguine

4 cups baby spinach

1 cup fresh or frozen (thawed) corn

2 scallions, thinly sliced, for garnish

1. Preheat the oven to 350°F.
2. Sauté the leeks in a large pot over medium heat for 5 minutes. Add water 1 to 2 tablespoons at a time to keep the leeks from sticking. Add the vegetable broth, kombu, shiitake mushrooms, ginger, tamari (if using), and cloves. Taste the broth, and if you think it needs more saltiness or depth of flavor, add more tamari, a little at a time, and taste again until the desired flavor is reached. Let the broth simmer until the mushrooms are tender, about 25 minutes.
3. While the broth is cooking, spread out the diced sweet potato on a nonstick baking sheet or a regular baking sheet lined with parchment paper. Season

with sea salt and black pepper to taste and bake until the potatoes are tender and starting to brown, 10 to 12 minutes.

4. Transfer 1 cup of the hot broth to a bowl and add the miso. Whisk it well to make a creamy consistency. Return the mixture to the pot. Discard the kombu.

5. Cook the noodles according to the package instructions and drain. Divide them among four large bowls and top each serving with 1 cup baby spinach and ¼ cup corn. Fill the bowls with the miso broth, garnish with the sliced scallions, and serve.

🍲 RECIPE TIP

Kombu is a dried seaweed that is used to add flavor to many dishes. You can find it in most natural food stores and Asian markets.

📝 NOTE FOR THE COOK

Be careful when measuring spices like ground cloves, because a little goes a long way. A pinch of cloves is equal to about 1/16 teaspoon.

📝 NOTE FOR THE COOK

The key to cutting potatoes safely is carefully cutting them in half so that they sit with stability on the work surface, and then cutting each half as you wish.

CURRIED LENTILS AND RICE

This dish is a variation of one I made throughout my college years, even though I was not vegan at the time. I made it because it was cheap, filling, and delicious. My version would start off simply at the beginning of the week as a beans and rice dish. The addition of vegetables came throughout the week to make the stew last longer. Cooking from scratch is a good way to teach kids about food budgets.

Serves 6

1 large yellow onion, diced

1 large carrot, peeled and diced

1 large celery stalk, diced

1 jalapeño pepper, seeded and minced

3 garlic cloves, minced

2 teaspoons grated fresh ginger

1 tablespoon curry powder

2 teaspoons ground cumin

2 teaspoons ground coriander

3 cups cooked brown basmati rice (page 106)

2 (15-ounce) cans green lentils, rinsed and drained, or 3 cups cooked green lentils

2 (12-ounce) bags frozen spinach, thawed and wrung dry

1 cup canned lite coconut milk

Grated zest and juice of 1 lemon

Sea salt

Chopped fresh cilantro, for garnish

1. Preheat the oven to 350°F.
2. Sauté the onion, carrot, and celery in a large saucepan over medium-high heat until the onion turns translucent and starts to brown, about 8 minutes. Add water 1 to 2 tablespoons at a time to keep the vegetables from sticking. Add the jalapeño, garlic, ginger, curry powder, cumin, and coriander, and cook until the spices are fragrant, about 1 minute.
3. Add the rice, lentils, spinach, coconut milk, and lemon zest and juice, and mix well. Season with sea salt to taste.
4. Transfer the mixture to a nonstick 9×13-inch baking pan. Bake until the stew is bubbly, 25 to 30 minutes. Let sit for 10 minutes, then garnish with chopped cilantro and serve.

RECIPE TIP

Brown basmati rice has more flavor than plain brown rice, but it can be more expensive. Use whatever rice or other grain will fit your budget.

TOFU YUNG

Egg foo yung was one of the first dishes I ate in a Chinese restaurant growing up, and it remains one of my favorites. This egg-free, oil-free version is a healthy go-to meal that kids love.

Serves 4

1 (12-ounce) package extra-firm silken tofu

2 tablespoons tamari, or to taste

¼ cup chickpea flour

2 tablespoons nutritional yeast

2 teaspoons double-acting baking powder

1 medium yellow onion, thinly sliced

8 ounces button mushrooms, sliced

2 cups chopped broccoli florets

2 cups fresh bean sprouts

1 recipe Good Gravy (page 102)

Chopped scallions, for garnish

4 cups cooked brown rice (page 106)

1. Preheat the oven to 350°F.
2. In a food processor, puree the silken tofu, tamari, chickpea flour, nutritional yeast, and baking powder. Transfer the mixture to a bowl and set aside.
3. In a large oven-safe nonstick skillet, stir-fry the onion, mushrooms, and broccoli florets over high heat until the onion starts to brown and the broccoli is just tender, about 5 minutes. Stir in the bean sprouts. Add the tofu mixture and mix well.
4. Lower the heat to medium and cook until the batter starts to bubble, about 5 minutes.
5. Transfer the pan to the oven and bake until the top of the omelet is lightly browned, 12 to 15 minutes.
6. Let the omelet sit for 5 minutes, then gently lift it around the edges with a spatula to loosen it from the pan. Turn out the omelet onto a serving

platter (if it does not loosen easily from the pan, gently push the spatula into the center of the pan until the omelet comes free) and top with the gravy. Garnish with the scallions and serve with the brown rice.

SAUSAGE, PEPPER, AND MUSHROOM PIZZA

Everyone likes pizza, and making pizza at home is a fun way to get the whole family involved in the kitchen. You can make three or four pizzas so family members can top theirs as they like. Making this healthy pizza crust from scratch takes a little effort, but it is almost impossible to find store-bought whole wheat pizza crust made without oil. Teaching kids how to make pizza dough from scratch is a fun way to get them into the kitchen, especially because they get to see the unbaked dough transform into the finished product.

Makes 2 (12-inch) pizzas

WHOLE WHEAT PIZZA CRUST

1 (¼-ounce) packet active dry yeast

1 tablespoon cane sugar, such as Sucanat

1 cup warm water (about 110°F)

½ teaspoon sea salt

About 2 cups whole wheat bread flour, divided

PIZZA

Cornmeal, for dusting

1 to 1½ cups pizza sauce

½ recipe Spicy Breakfast Patties (page 56), crumbled

1 large yellow onion, diced

1 large green bell pepper, seeded and diced

8 ounces button mushrooms, sliced

Sea salt and black pepper

1 recipe Cheese Sauce (page 98)

Chopped fresh basil, for garnish

1. To make the pizza crust, in a large bowl, whisk together the yeast, sugar, and warm water. Let the mixture sit until it starts to foam, then add the sea salt, and, using a whisk, stir in 1 cup of the flour. Beat the dough for 75 strokes. Add as much of the remaining 1 cup flour as needed to make a dough that is stiff but still a little tacky to the touch. Cover the dough with plastic wrap and let it sit in a warm place until it has doubled in volume, about 45 minutes. Punch it down and let it rise again, about 20 minutes.

2. During the last rise, preheat the oven to 425°F.

3. To make the pizza, dust two 12-inch pizza pans or baking sheets with cornmeal.

4. Divide the pizza dough in half and shape each half into a round. Press the pizza dough onto each pizza pan or baking sheet. Spread half of the pizza sauce over each dough and distribute half of each of the toppings over the sauce. Season with sea salt and black pepper to taste. Spoon the cheese sauce over the vegetables.

5. Bake until the crust is browned, 12 to 13 minutes. Remove the pizza from the oven and garnish with the chopped basil. Serve.

🍽 RECIPE TIP

Bake one pizza to have now and freeze the other half of the dough for a future meal.

TWICE-BAKED SAMOSA POTATOES

Samosas are popular East Indian appetizers usually filled with potatoes, peas, and warm spices. In this version, the filling is stuffed into a baked potato, making it a complete meal. If your family is new to Indian cuisine, pull out a map and show them where this dish originated.

Serves 4

4 large russet potatoes

1 (12-ounce) package extra-firm silken tofu

1 medium yellow onion, diced small

1 jalapeño pepper, seeded and minced

1 tablespoon grated fresh ginger

¼ cup finely chopped fresh cilantro

2 teaspoons black mustard seeds, toasted

1 teaspoon garam masala

1 teaspoon ground coriander

1 teaspoon ground cumin

1 cup green peas

Sea salt

1. Preheat the oven to 350°F.
2. Scrub the potatoes well and pierce each a few times with a fork. Place them on a baking sheet and bake until tender, about 1 hour.
3. While the potatoes bake, puree the silken tofu in a blender until smooth. Set aside.
4. Sauté the onion in a large saucepan over medium heat until it turns translucent and starts to brown, about 8 minutes. Add water 1 to 2 tablespoons at a time to keep the onion from sticking. Reduce the heat to medium-low and add the jalapeño, ginger, cilantro, mustard seeds, garam masala, coriander, and cumin. Cook for 4 minutes, then remove the pan from the heat. Add the peas and pureed silken tofu. Season with sea salt to taste and mix well.

5. When the potatoes are tender, let them cool until they are easily handled. Cut each potato in half lengthwise and scoop out all but a ½-inch wall of the flesh. Add the scooped potato flesh to the pan with the tofu mixture and mix well.
6. Spoon the filling into each of the baked potato halves and place them back on the baking sheet. Bake until the tops of the potatoes are browned, 25 to 30 minutes. Serve.

TWICE-BAKED SWEET POTATOES

You can teach your family about fusion cooking with this recipe, which features combinations that aren't necessarily traditional to any one cuisine. I've never had Twice-Baked Sweet Potatoes in an Indian restaurant, but I wouldn't mind if they borrowed my idea.

Serves 4

4 large sweet potatoes (about 2 pounds)

½ medium yellow onion, diced small

½ medium red bell pepper, seeded and diced small

2 garlic cloves, minced

2 teaspoons curry powder

1 cup frozen or fresh green peas

1 cup cooked or canned chickpeas

½ cup toasted cashews (see Note on page 43)

½ cup chopped fresh cilantro

Sea salt

1 recipe Sour Cream (page 94)

_____

1. Preheat the oven to 350°F.
2. Scrub the sweet potatoes well and pierce each a few times with a fork. Place them on a baking sheet and bake until tender, 45 to 60 minutes.
3. While the potatoes bake, sauté the onion and bell pepper in a skillet over medium heat until the onion turns translucent and starts to brown, about 8 minutes. Add the garlic and curry powder and cook for another minute. Add the green peas, chickpeas, cashews, and cilantro, and cook for 2 to 3 more minutes to marry the flavors.
4. When the sweet potatoes are tender, let them cool until they are easily handled. Cut each sweet potato in half lengthwise and scoop out all but a ½-inch wall of the flesh. Add the scooped sweet potato flesh to the pan with the chickpea mixture. Season with sea salt to taste and mix well.
5. Spoon the filling into each of the sweet potato halves and place them back on the baking sheet. Bake until the tops of the sweet potatoes start to brown, about 25 minutes. Serve with the sour cream.

At Home with the Plant-Based Family

LEANNE CAMPBELL

The China Study Cookbook author, LeAnne Campbell, daughter of T. Colin Campbell, was raised on a meat-and-potatoes diet, helping her mom prepare these foods in the kitchen. When her father started bringing home the results of his research, her family slowly began cutting out meat, but the transition to a whole foods, plant-based diet didn't happen overnight. LeAnne did not experience the difference until she came home after her first year of college. Her family had completely cut out meat and most dairy and other animal proteins. "The last to go in the house was ice cream. That was a hard one," LeAnne jokes.

During college, LeAnne worked in her father's lab, proportioning lab samples and conducting research for what would become known as *The China Study*. After graduating, she joined the Peace Corps and traveled to the Dominican Republic, after which she went vegetarian. Her experience abroad solidified this decision because she had witnessed firsthand the malnourishment that many men, women, and children face around the world. "It really got me thinking about issues of sustainability and food production," she says. "Everyone could have food if we ate a plant-based diet."

While in the Dominican Republic, LeAnne also discovered another passion: rice and beans. Rice and beans is LeAnne's go-to when cooking for herself and her kids, who call the classic dish their "comfort food."

Wanting her children to feel comfortable with this type of lifestyle, LeAnne educated them about a plant-based lifestyle, including the health, ethical, and environmental reasons for doing so. They ultimately became just as dedicated to this lifestyle as she is. "Nelson and Steven would share their food with other kids when they were younger. They never felt peer pressure from others about what they were eating," she recalls. "And we were always respectful when we were somewhere that didn't have too many plant-based options." One way she increased her sons' enthusiasm about eating plant-based was by making a menu every week for them to look at. "They were always involved in helping me decide what we would eat during the week."

As a mother earning her PhD and working full time, LeAnne was able to stick to the diet because of the support from her children and her constant planning. A fan of batch cooking, she would utilize big casserole dishes and bake large batches for the whole family. "I would make a big pan of lasagna, and if they could, they would have eaten the whole pan," LeAnne recalls. "They were healthy eaters with big appetites, so I always had to take out their lunch portions before I let them eat!"

Ensuring her kids were able to eat plant-based away from home provided consistency that helped form good habits for the future, and thanks to LeAnne's work when they were young, Steven, a college graduate, and Nelson, now in college, now shop, cook, and eat plant-based all on their own, and they have thrived and continue to thrive on this diet. ⌐◯⌐

CASSEROLES

ZESTY CORNBREAD CASSEROLE

My dad used to make a version of this dish with bacon and baked beans. It was tasty but not healthy. This version is both tasty and healthy.

Serves 6 to 8

1 medium yellow onion, diced

1 medium red bell pepper, seeded and diced

1 medium green bell pepper, seeded and diced

1 jalapeño pepper, seeded and minced

2 garlic cloves, minced

1 tablespoon mild chili powder

2 teaspoons ground cumin

2 teaspoons dried oregano

1 (12-ounce) bag frozen corn, thawed, or 2 cups fresh corn

1 (15-ounce) can black beans, rinsed and drained, or 1½ cups cooked black beans

Sea salt and black pepper

2 cups cornmeal

2 cups whole wheat pastry flour

1 tablespoon double-acting baking powder

2 cups unsweetened applesauce

2 cups unsweetened plant milk

1. Preheat the oven to 350°F.
2. Sauté the onion, bell peppers, and jalapeño in a skillet over medium-high heat until the onion turns translucent and starts to brown, about 8 minutes. Add water 1 to 2 tablespoons at a time to keep the vegetables from sticking. Add the garlic, chili powder, cumin, and oregano, and cook for another minute to toast the spices.
3. Add the corn and black beans, season with sea salt and black pepper to taste, and cook for 5 minutes to let the flavors marry. Set aside.
4. In a mixing bowl, whisk together the cornmeal, flour, baking powder, and ½ teaspoon sea salt. Make a well in the center of the flour mixture and add the applesauce, plant milk, and sautéed vegetable mixture. Fold the ingredients together and pour the batter into a nonstick 9×13-inch baking dish.
5. Bake until a toothpick inserted in the center of the cornbread comes out clean, 40 to 45 minutes. Let cool before slicing and serving.

RICE AND VEGGIE CASSEROLE

You can make this casserole different every time by substituting other vegetables and trying a different grain like quinoa for a change of pace. Let the kids decide which vegetables and grain they want to use. It's a great lesson in teaching versatility in cooking.

Serves 8

2 large yellow onions, diced

3 celery stalks, sliced

2 large red bell peppers, seeded and diced

2 (12-ounce) bags frozen broccoli florets

2 (12-ounce) bags frozen corn

2 teaspoons dried sage

4 cups cooked brown rice (page 106)

Sea salt and black pepper

2 recipes Cheese Sauce (page 98)

1. Preheat the oven to 350°F.
2. Sauté the onions, celery, and bell peppers in a large skillet over medium heat until the onions turn translucent and start to brown, about 8 minutes. Add water 1 to 2 tablespoons at a time to keep the vegetables from sticking.
3. Add the broccoli, corn, and sage, and cook until the broccoli is just tender, about 4 minutes. Add the rice, season with sea salt and black pepper to taste, and cook for another 3 minutes.
4. Add the cheese sauce and mix well. Pour the mixture into a nonstick 9×13-inch baking pan and bake until bubbly, about 30 minutes. Let the casserole sit for 10 minutes before serving.

 RECIPE TIP

Feel free to substitute different vegetables from the ones suggested here, but be sure to use the same amount called for.

JOHNNY MARZETTI

This casserole originated in my hometown of Columbus, Ohio, at the Marzetti family restaurant. The restaurant is no longer there, but my memories of this Italian American dish go right back to my school, where it was often on the cafeteria menu.

Serves 8

12 ounces whole-grain macaroni

2 medium yellow onions, roughly chopped

8 ounces button mushrooms, sliced

3 garlic cloves, minced

1 teaspoon dried oregano

1 (28-ounce) can diced tomatoes, undrained

1 recipe Spicy Breakfast Patties (page 56), crumbled

Sea salt and black pepper

1 recipe Cheese Sauce (page 98)

½ cup whole-grain bread crumbs

1. Preheat the oven to 350°F.
2. Prepare the macaroni according to package instructions, drain, and set aside.
3. While the pasta is cooking, sauté the onions and mushrooms in a large saucepan over medium-high heat until the onions turn translucent and start to brown, about 8 minutes. Add water 1 to 2 tablespoons at a time to keep the vegetables from sticking. Add the garlic and oregano and cook until fragrant, about 1 minute.
4. Add the tomatoes, cover, and reduce the heat to medium-low. Cook until the sauce thickens, about 15 minutes.
5. Add the crumbled breakfast patties and drained noodles to the pan and gently mix until all the ingredients are well incorporated. Season with sea salt and black pepper to taste.
6. Spoon the noodle mixture into a nonstick 9×13-inch baking dish. Pour the cheese sauce over the noodle mixture and spread it evenly over the surface. Sprinkle the bread crumbs over the cheese sauce. Bake until bubbly and browned, 25 to 30 minutes. Let sit for 10 minutes before serving.

MAC AND CHEESE

It is rare to find a kid who doesn't like mac and cheese. It is an icon of favorite kid foods, up there with pizza and hot dogs. This plant-based version comes together quickly.

Serves 6 to 8

12 ounces whole-grain macaroni

1 recipe Cheese Sauce (page 98)

1 cup whole-grain bread crumbs (optional)

1. Preheat the oven to 350°F.
2. Prepare the macaroni according to the package instructions. Drain and transfer to a large mixing bowl. Add the cheese sauce and mix well. Pour the mixture into a nonstick 9×13-inch baking dish. Top with the bread crumbs, if desired.
3. Bake until the bread crumbs are browned and the sauce is bubbly around the edges, 25 to 30 minutes.

🍽 RECIPE TIP

You can make a quick stovetop version of this dish by heating the cheese sauce in a large saucepan and adding the cooked macaroni to the pan. Mix well and serve.

CHILI MAC AND CHEESE CASSEROLE

This casserole is really two dishes made into one, and though you could easily serve them separately, this casserole is a little more festive than a couple of side dishes would be. Kids will love it however you serve it because they just love mac and cheese. Luckily, since casseroles are easy to freeze, you can always have one on hand to feed a crowd.

Serves 8

1 recipe Lentil Chili (page 179)
1 recipe Mac and Cheese (page 224)

1. Preheat the oven to 350°F.
2. Spoon the chili into a nonstick 9×13-inch baking dish. Spoon the mac and cheese over the chili to cover it completely.
3. Bake until the mac and cheese is browned and the dish is bubbly, 25 to 35 minutes.

 RECIPE TIP

If you've prepared your chili and mac and cheese fresh and they are still warm, you won't need to cook this dish for the full 35 minutes. Instead, turn the oven up to 375°F and bake it for about 15 minutes.

MEDITERRANEAN LOAF

I often tell the story of how my divorced parents would frequently both cook meatloaf the same week: Mom during the week, and Dad on the weekend. It happened often enough that for a long time I did not want meatloaf—ever! My mom would, on occasion, make an Italian meatloaf with a ricotta filling. This is my ode to that dish but with a healthier and still tasty twist.

Serves 6 to 8

2 recipes Meatballs (page 199), prepared but not formed into meatballs or baked

2 pounds russet potatoes, scrubbed and diced

2 cups fresh basil leaves, finely chopped

1 cup sun-dried tomatoes, finely chopped

Sea salt and black pepper

1. Preheat the oven to 350°F.
2. Press the meatball mixture into the bottom of a nonstick loaf pan. Set aside.
3. Put the potatoes in a pot and cover with cold water. Bring the water to a boil over high heat, reduce the heat to medium, and simmer the potatoes until tender, 10 to 12 minutes. Drain the potatoes, reserving 1½ cups of the cooking liquid.
4. Return the potatoes to the pot and mash them, adding enough of the reserved cooking liquid to keep them from being gummy. Add the basil and sun-dried tomatoes and mix well. Season with sea salt and black pepper to taste. Spoon the potatoes over the meatball mixture.
5. Bake for 30 minutes. Let sit for 10 minutes before serving.

🍽 RECIPE TIP

The secret to perfect fat-free mashed potatoes is to leave some of the cooking water in the pan with the potatoes when you mash them. Start with a small amount of water and add more as needed to get the consistency you like.

SWEET POTATO AND BASMATI RICE CASSEROLE

If your family is new to Indian cooking, this is a great starter recipe. The flavors are mild, and the sweet and savory combination is popular with taste buds of all ages.

Serves 6 to 8

1 large yellow onion, diced

1 red bell pepper, seeded and diced

3 garlic cloves, minced

1 tablespoon curry powder

1 teaspoon ground coriander

¼ teaspoon black pepper

2 cups low-sodium vegetable broth

2 large sweet potatoes, peeled and diced

1 (15-ounce) can lite coconut milk

3 cups cooked brown basmati rice (page 106)

1 cup golden raisins

1 cup whole-grain bread crumbs

1 teaspoon garlic powder

½ teaspoon ground fennel seed

1. Preheat the oven to 375°F.
2. Sauté the onion and bell pepper in a skillet over medium heat until the onion turns translucent and starts to brown, about 8 minutes. Add water 1 to 2 tablespoons at a time to keep the vegetables from sticking. Add the garlic, curry powder, coriander, and black pepper, and cook for another minute.
3. Add the vegetable broth and sweet potatoes and cook until the sweet potatoes are just tender, about 5 minutes. Add the coconut milk, cooked rice, and golden raisins, and mix well. Spoon the mixture into a nonstick 9×13-inch baking dish.
4. Combine the bread crumbs, garlic powder, and fennel in a small bowl, and mix well. Sprinkle the bread crumb mixture over the casserole and bake until the bread crumbs have browned and the casserole is bubbly, 20 to 25 minutes. Let sit for 5 minutes before serving.

📝 NOTE FOR THE COOK

The key to cutting potatoes safely is carefully cutting them in half so that they sit with stability on the work surface, and then cutting each half as you wish.

AUTUMN VEGETABLE POT PIE WITH BISCUIT CRUST

My first pot pie was a frozen store-bought version, and I loved it. I finally had a homemade pot pie at my first restaurant job and never had store-bought again. By cooking with your kids and teaching them to cook, you can show them how much better homemade tastes than store-bought.

Serves 6 to 8

1 large head cauliflower, cut into florets, or 1 pound frozen cauliflower florets

4 cups low-sodium vegetable broth

2 large leeks, light green and white parts, thinly sliced

2 large carrots, peeled and chopped

1 large sweet potato, peeled and chopped

1 large turnip, peeled and diced

1 (12-ounce) bag frozen green peas

2 tablespoons nutritional yeast

2 teaspoons dried thyme

½ teaspoon ground nutmeg

Sea salt and black pepper

1 recipe Biscuits (page 50), unbaked

1. Combine the cauliflower and vegetable broth in a large saucepan, bring to a boil over medium-high heat, and cook the cauliflower until very tender, 8 to 10 minutes. Using a slotted spoon, transfer the cauliflower to a blender and puree, using as much of the vegetable broth as needed to make a creamy sauce. (Reserve the remaining vegetable broth.) You may need to do this in batches.

2. Sauté the leeks and carrots in a large saucepan over medium heat until the leeks start to brown, about 8 minutes. Add water 1 to 2 tablespoons at a time to keep the vegetables from sticking.

3. Add the sweet potato, turnip, frozen peas, nutritional yeast, thyme, nutmeg, and 2 cups of the vegetable broth from the cauliflower. Mix well and simmer

until the vegetables are tender, about 15 minutes. Season with sea salt and black pepper to taste.

4. Add the cauliflower puree to the pan and mix well. Spoon the mixture into a nonstick 9×13-inch baking pan. Bake for 20 minutes.

5. Use a medium ice cream scoop or a ⅓-cup measure to form about eight biscuits from the unbaked dough. Top the pot pie with the biscuits and bake until the biscuits are brown and firm to the touch, 20 to 25 minutes.

📝 NOTE FOR THE COOK

The key to cutting potatoes safely is carefully cutting them in half so that they sit with stability on the work surface, and then cutting each half as you wish.

TORTILLA PIE

Parents around the world know that comfort food soothes the soul. My dad made more dishes like this tortilla pie than my mom did, but we were happy to have it no matter who prepared it.

Serves 6 to 8

2 cups water

1 cup millet

1 medium yellow onion, diced

1 large poblano pepper, diced

4 garlic cloves, minced

1 tablespoon ground cumin

1 tablespoon dried basil

2 teaspoons dried oregano

1 (12-ounce) package frozen corn

¼ cup tomato puree

Sea salt and black pepper

1 package whole-grain tortillas

1 (15-ounce) can fat-free vegan refried beans

1 (15-ounce) jar salsa verde

1 recipe Cheese Sauce (page 98)

Chopped scallions, for garnish

Chopped cilantro, for garnish

1. Bring the water to a boil over high heat in a large saucepan and add the millet. Return the water to a boil, cover, and reduce the heat to medium. Cook for 20 minutes, or until the millet is very tender.
2. While the millet cooks, sauté the onion and poblano pepper over medium heat in a large saucepan until the onion turns translucent and starts to brown, about 8 minutes. Add water 1 to 2 tablespoons at a time to keep the vegetables from sticking. Add the garlic, cumin, basil, and oregano, and cook another minute.

3. Add the corn and tomato puree and remove the pan from the heat. Add the cooked millet, season with sea salt and black pepper to taste, and let cool.
4. When the millet is cool enough to handle, use a spatula to crumble it.
5. Preheat the oven to 425°F.
6. Place a layer of tortillas in the bottom of a 10-inch pie pan. Spread ½ cup refried beans over the tortillas and ½ cup salsa verde over the refried beans.
7. Sprinkle a third of the millet mixture over the salsa verde, and spoon a quarter of the cheese sauce over the millet mixture.
8. Add another layer of tortillas, ½ cup refried beans, ½ cup salsa verde, and another third of the millet mixture. Top the millet again with another quarter of the cheese sauce.
9. Repeat the process one more time with the tortillas, refried beans, salsa verde, millet mixture, and cheese sauce; add a final layer of tortillas; and then top with the remaining cheese sauce.
10. Bake for 20 to 25 minutes, until the top is lightly browned. Let cool 10 minutes before serving. Serve garnished with the scallions and cilantro.

📝 NOTE FOR THE COOK

This recipe is not as daunting as it looks. Keep in mind that some of the items are prepared for you, such as the salsa verde and refried beans, and that other items on the list are used for garnish and take little time to prepare. Don't forget to practice *mise en place* by making your cheese sauce and gathering your other ingredients together ahead of time!

📝 NOTE FOR THE COOK

For the millet to work as a binder (to hold everything together in a patty) in this dish, you need to almost overcook it. If it seems crumbly when you first make it, add 2 to 3 tablespoons more water to the pan, cover tightly, and let it cook for another 2 to 3 minutes. The millet should hold together when pinched between your fingers or pressed against the side of the pan.

At Home with the Plant-Based Family

PAM FROST

I first met Pam Frost when she attended one of my cooking classes in 2010. A mom of six, Pam delved into the world of plant-based eating after reading a few books on the subject. She decided she wanted to give the lifestyle a try, never having been a particular fan of meat anyway, and changed her diet virtually overnight.

"I have always been pretty healthy," Pam says. "Never loved meat, never hated it. I just ate it because it was there, growing up. I always ate lots of vegetables instead, and huge salads. I read a couple of books and kept thinking if I was sick, I could do this. I started thinking, why don't I just do it anyway? It's healthier. So I kind of did it overnight. I just decided I'm going to try this and see what happens and then never looked back."

Often eating five or six smaller meals a day instead of a larger three, Pam originally called her change in diet "eating healthy" and didn't put pressure on her husband and kids to follow in her footsteps. But her family was "totally supportive," according to Pam, and after watching her lose roughly twenty pounds, each member started making their own healthy changes to their diet.

"My oldest daughter is somewhat vegan and doing pretty well with it, and my husband's given up dairy for the most part. My youngest daughter has gone vegetarian, and all of my boys—they've always been big vege-table eaters and they'll text me pictures of a vegan pizza that they bought at the store or kale chips that they had. They like to show me their healthy things," Pam boasts.

A grandmother of four, Pam has more energy than most people half her age thanks in part to eating plant-based. When asked what advice she has for any-one else living on a plant-based diet, Pam has this to say: "Don't become too stressed or overwhelmed with it. Take it easy, and if you find out something had chicken broth in it or something, just try to relax about it. Make the transition to a plant-based diet slowly if need be, and don't be afraid to try lots of different things that you've never tried before"—like the tofu and mushrooms she's become a fan of since transitioning to a plant-based diet.

And the best way to get the rest of your family on board? It might just be to lead, like Pam, by example.

DESSERTS

DATE PUREE

I use this puree in a lot of dessert recipes. It is a great way to get your family off processed sugar.

Makes 3 cups

2 cups pitted dates
2 cups water

1. Combine the dates and water in a small saucepan. Cover and cook over medium heat until the dates are tender, about 10 minutes. Drain and reserve the cooking water.
2. Puree the dates in a blender, adding just enough water to make a creamy consistency. Let cool to room temperature, then store in an airtight container for up to a week.

 RECIPE TIP

Add as little water as possible to the dates to concentrate the sweetness in the puree. Date puree is not a 1:1 replacement for sugar and, to the newbie, may not taste as sweet. If you are trying to use this date puree instead of sugar in your favorite recipes, you may need to cut back a bit on the liquid in your recipe, and it may take a little experimentation to figure out exactly how much date puree to use.

VANILLA-ALMOND DESSERT SAUCE

This dessert sauce tastes great over fresh berries, granola, or even Pancakes (page 45).

Makes 2 cups

1 (12-ounce) package extra-firm silken tofu

¾ cup Date Puree (page 241)

2 tablespoons almond or cashew butter (optional)

1 teaspoon pure vanilla extract

1 teaspoon almond extract

Pinch sea salt (optional)

Combine all the ingredients in a food processor and puree until smooth and creamy. Store in an airtight container in the refrigerator for up to a week.

 RECIPE TIP

Many recipes in this book call for your choice of silken tofu or canned white beans. This is one recipe where beans don't make a good substitute for the tofu.

CHOCOLATE-COVERED PEANUT BUTTER–FILLED DATES

Kids love getting messy making these treats. If you don't have a piping bag, it is worth getting one to stuff the peanut butter into the dates. You can buy disposable ones at most grocery stores. I like to have chocolate as a special treat every now and then, but you can omit the chocolate for a sugar-free treat.

Makes 24 dates

1 cup creamy peanut butter

24 plump Medjool dates, pitted

1 (10-ounce) bag vegan chocolate chips (see Tip)

1. Fill a piping bag with the peanut butter and fill each date with some of the peanut butter. (If you don't have a piping bag, you can use a teaspoon.) Place the filled dates on a baking sheet and freeze for 15 minutes.
2. Melt the chocolate chips in a double boiler.
3. Dip each filled date in the chocolate using a fork and then place back on the baking sheet.
4. Refrigerate the dates until the chocolate is set, about 15 minutes. Store in an airtight container in the refrigerator.

 RECIPE TIP

To melt chocolate chips, place some water in a small saucepan and place a bowl on top of the pan. Add the chocolate chips to the bowl and let them warm until melted, 5 to 6 minutes. Do not stir them much, if at all, as they can become gritty.

CHOCOLATE SWEET POTATO HUMMUS

This recipe is a great way to add vegetables into the family diet. It has a great flavor and is easy to make. Don't tell, don't let them see your recipe, and they won't know it's a healthy treat. You can also use this as a frosting, for example in place of the frosting recipe for Chocolate Doughnuts (page 47).

Serves 6

2 large sweet potatoes

1 cup Date Puree (page 241)

¼ cup creamy peanut butter or other nut butter

3 tablespoons unsweetened cocoa powder

1 teaspoon pure vanilla extract

Pinch sea salt

1. Preheat the oven to 350°F.
2. Scrub the sweet potatoes well and pierce each a few times with a fork. Place them on a baking sheet and bake until tender, 45 to 60 minutes. Let the sweet potatoes cool to room temperature.
3. Cut the sweet potatoes in half and scrape the flesh into a food processor. Add the remaining ingredients and puree until smooth and creamy. Store in an airtight container in the refrigerator for up to a week.

 RECIPE TIP

There are two tricks for getting this hummus creamy. One is to make sure the sweet potatoes are well cooked. Check them by sticking a fork in the thickest part of the potato. If the fork does not go in easily, put them back in the oven and keep roasting until they are tender. The second trick is to puree them in the food processor long enough to remove all the lumps.

CHOCOLATE POPS

These freezer pops taste better than any I had as a kid, and without all the sugar of the traditional version.

Makes 7 ice pops

1 cup unsweetened plant milk

1 (10-ounce) bag unsweetened vegan dark chocolate chips

1 cup Date Puree (page 241), or more to taste

1. Warm the plant milk in a small saucepan over medium heat, but do not let it boil. When the milk is steaming, add the chocolate chips and remove the pan from the heat. Let it sit until the chocolate chips melt, about 5 minutes.
2. Once the chocolate chips are melted, transfer the mixture to a blender, add the date puree, and process until smooth and creamy.
3. Spoon the puree into freezer pop molds, cover, and place craft sticks in the molds. Freeze until firm, about 3 hours.
4. To remove the pops from the molds, rinse the molds under cool water for 30 seconds, remove the lid, and gently pull the pops from the molds. Serve immediately, or store frozen in zip-top bags.

 RECIPE TIP

Removing the pops from the molds can take a little effort and a little patience. The first time I made freezer pops I thought that hot water was the best way to get the pops out of the mold. Instead, it made a mess. Practice patience in the kitchen and teach your kids the same. You will be rewarded with a better treat for your efforts.

CHEESECAKE POPS

I grew up in a neighborhood where the ice cream truck was a staple visitor in the summer months. If I could find an ice cream truck that served this delicious treat, the kid in me would go running for the truck today.

Makes 9 ice pops

½ cup raw cashews

1 cup Medjool dates, pitted

1 cup strawberries, blueberries, or raspberries, fresh or frozen

2 tablespoons fresh lemon juice

1. Put the cashews and dates in a bowl, cover with water, and soak for at least 4 hours or overnight.
2. Drain and reserve the soaking liquid. Transfer the cashews and dates to a blender, along with the berries and lemon juice. Puree until smooth and creamy, adding enough of the soaking liquid to make a creamy consistency.
3. Spoon the puree into freezer pop molds, cover, and place craft sticks in the molds. Freeze until firm, about 3 hours.
4. To remove the pops from the molds, rinse the molds under cool water for 30 seconds, remove the lid, and gently pull the pops from the molds. Serve immediately, or store frozen in zip-top bags.

🍽 RECIPE TIP

To make vanilla cheesecake pops, leave out the berries and add 2 tablespoons more cashews, ¼ cup water, and 1 teaspoon pure vanilla extract to the blender.

🍽 RECIPE TIP

Removing the pops from the molds can take a little effort and a little patience. The first time I made freezer pops I thought that hot water was the best way to get the pops out of the mold. Instead, it made a mess. Practice patience in the kitchen and teach your kids the same. You will be rewarded with a better treat for your efforts.

 RECIPE TIP

Sugar-free desserts may not taste sweet enough for those first starting to eat a healthier diet. It can take several weeks for your taste buds to down-regulate. If your kids, or you, are not enjoying sugar-free choices like this one, start by replacing half of the dates with an equal amount of maple syrup and then slowly reducing the amount of maple syrup while increasing the amount of dates in subsequent batches.

CHUNKY MONKEY COOKIES

I have loved chocolate and peanut butter together since I was a kid and ate my first candy bar with that combination. If you and the kids are also fans, try using these cookies in the Whoopie Pie recipe on page 262.

Makes about 16 cookies

1 cup cooked or canned white beans (see Tip)

2 ripe bananas

⅔ cup creamy peanut butter

1 cup Date Puree (page 241)

1 tablespoon pure vanilla extract

1 cup whole wheat pastry flour

2 teaspoons double-acting baking powder

½ teaspoon sea salt

½ cup vegan chocolate chips

1. Preheat the oven to 350°F.
2. Combine the beans, bananas, peanut butter, date puree, and vanilla in a food processor, and puree until smooth.
3. In a large mixing bowl, whisk together the flour, baking powder, and sea salt. Add the chocolate chips and mix well. Add the banana mixture to the flour mixture and gently fold together.
4. Using an ice cream scoop or ¼-cup measure, shape the cookies and place them on a nonstick baking sheet. Press down on each one gently to flatten it.
5. Bake for about 12 minutes, until the cookies are slightly browned and firm to the touch.

 RECIPE TIP

Any white beans will work in this recipe—Great Northern, cannellini, or navy—so use whatever you have on hand.

LIVING THE DREAM BROWNIES

When I owned my vegan bakery, I used to make a brownie that was so rich and full of fat that if you put one on a paper towel, it would soak right through. Parents were scared to give a whole brownie to their kids for fear of what might happen. This version is much healthier than that one but still a treat.

Makes 18 brownies

1½ cups spelt flour

2 teaspoons double-acting baking powder

¼ teaspoon sea salt

½ cup unsweetened cocoa powder

2 tablespoons ground flax seed

6 tablespoons water

¾ cup pure maple syrup

¾ cup unsweetened applesauce

2 teaspoons pure vanilla extract

½ cup vegan chocolate chips

½ cup finely chopped, lightly toasted walnuts (see Note on page 43)

1. Preheat the oven to 350°F.
2. In a mixing bowl, whisk together the spelt flour, baking powder, sea salt, and cocoa powder.
3. In a blender, puree the flax seed and water. Transfer to another mixing bowl. Add the maple syrup, applesauce, and vanilla extract.
4. Add the flour mixture to the maple syrup mixture, along with the chocolate chips and walnuts, and gently fold everything together.
5. Spoon the batter into a nonstick 9×13-inch baking pan and bake until a toothpick inserted into the center comes out clean, 25 to 30 minutes. Cool to room temperature before cutting.

 RECIPE TIP

Flax seeds blended with water make a good egg replacer in baked goods.

OAT AND APRICOT BARS

These fruit and grain bars are free of processed sugar and full of flavor. They make a great snack on the road when healthy options are hard to find, and they are also one of the least messy treats you can give the kids in the car.

Makes 9 bars

3 cups rolled oats

1½ cups chopped pitted dates

¾ cup unsweetened applesauce

1½ teaspoons pure vanilla extract (optional)

¾ teaspoon ground cinnamon

¼ teaspoon sea salt (optional)

1½ cups dried unsulfured apricots

1 cup water, or more as needed

Grated zest of ½ orange

---

1. Preheat the oven to 350°F.
2. Combine the oats, dates, applesauce, vanilla (if using), cinnamon, and sea salt (if using) in a food processor, and process until the mixture forms a cohesive ball. Remove the dough from the processor and press two-thirds of it into the bottom of a nonstick 9-inch square baking pan. Bake for 10 minutes, then set aside to cool for 10 minutes.
3. Meanwhile, combine the apricots, water, and orange zest in a small saucepan, and cook over medium-low heat until most of the water has evaporated and the apricots are tender, about 15 minutes. Transfer the apricots and any remaining water to the food processor and puree until smooth and creamy, 3 to 4 minutes.
4. Spread the apricot puree over the cooled crust. Crumble the remaining dough over the apricot puree and bake for another 10 minutes. Let cool to room temperature before cutting into 9 bars. Store in an airtight container in the refrigerator for up to 5 days.

RECIPE TIP

You can replace the apricots with dates for a different flavor. Add 1 teaspoon ground cinnamon and use 1 teaspoon pure vanilla extract instead of the orange zest.

APPLE PECAN FIG BARS

My mom used to make a fresh apple cookie that was more like a cake than a cookie. This bar is an ode to that treat. Thanks, Mom!

Makes 9 bars

1 cup cooked or canned white beans (see Tip)

1 cup Date Puree (page 241)

1 Granny Smith apple, peeled, cored, and grated

2 tablespoons arrowroot powder

1 teaspoon pure vanilla extract

½ cup unsweetened applesauce

¾ cup spelt flour

1 teaspoon double-acting baking powder

¼ teaspoon sea salt

1 teaspoon ground cinnamon

¼ teaspoon ground nutmeg

1 cup chopped dried figs

½ cup finely chopped toasted pecans (see Note on page 43)

1. Preheat the oven to 350°F.
2. Combine the beans and date puree in a food processor and puree until smooth and creamy. Transfer the bean mixture to a mixing bowl and add the grated apple, arrowroot powder, vanilla, and applesauce. Mix well.
3. In a small bowl, whisk together the spelt flour, baking powder, sea salt, cinnamon, and nutmeg. Add the flour mixture to the bowl with the bean mixture, along with the figs and pecans, and fold the ingredients together.
4. Spoon the batter into a nonstick 8-inch square baking dish, and gently press the batter into the pan. Bake until a toothpick inserted into the center comes out clean, 35 to 40 minutes. Let stand for at least 20 minutes before cutting into 9 bars.

 **RECIPE TIP**

Any white beans will work in this recipe—Great Northern, cannellini, or navy—so use whatever you have on hand.

PUMPKIN BARS

My mom's pumpkin bread recipe is so good that downtown restaurants used to pay her to make it for them to sell. Her bread was moist, spicy, and not too sweet, and whenever she made it, we ate it like we were never going to see it again. This is my ode to her bread in bar form.

Makes 16 bars

1 cup 100% pumpkin puree (not pumpkin pie filling)

¾ cup pure maple syrup

¼ cup unsweetened applesauce

1 teaspoon pure vanilla extract

2 cups whole wheat pastry flour

4 teaspoons double-acting baking powder

¼ teaspoon sea salt

2 teaspoons ground cinnamon

1 teaspoon ground ginger

Pinch ground cloves (see Note on page 179)

1 cup chopped walnuts or pecans (optional)

1. Preheat the oven to 350°F. Line an 8-inch square baking pan with parchment paper.
2. In a large mixing bowl, whisk together the pumpkin puree, maple syrup, applesauce, and vanilla.
3. In another bowl, whisk together the flour, baking powder, sea salt, cinnamon, ginger, and cloves. Pour the pumpkin mixture into the bowl with the flour mixture, add the nuts (if using), and use a wooden spoon or spatula to gently fold the ingredients together. Do not overmix.
4. Spoon the batter into the prepared pan and gently press the batter into the pan. Bake until a toothpick inserted into the center comes out clean, 35 to 40 minutes. Let stand for at least 20 minutes before cutting into 16 squares.

RECIPE TIP

Many of the dessert recipes in this cookbook call for date puree as the primary sweetener. But because the pumpkin puree is so dense, using date puree here—another dense ingredient—would make the pumpkin bars too heavy.

RECIPE TIP

Teach kids how to make their own pumpkin puree: Bake a whole pie pumpkin for an hour in a 350°F oven, then let it cool to room temperature. Peel it, remove the seeds, and then puree it in batches in a food processor. It is a great lesson to show that many things that come from a can are easily—and more cheaply—made from scratch.

WHOOPIE PIES

Whoopie pies are traditionally made of two small cakes with a creamy filling. I make an unusual version here using my favorite breakfast spread as the filling, with happy results. If you are allergic to nuts, simply omit them from the filling.

Makes 9 pies

2 cups whole wheat pastry flour

½ cup unsweetened cocoa powder

1 tablespoon double-acting baking powder

¼ teaspoon sea salt

1 cup unsweetened applesauce

1 cup unsweetened plant milk

½ cup pure maple syrup

1 teaspoon pure vanilla extract

1 recipe Breakfast Spread (page 53)

1. Preheat the oven to 350°F.
2. In a mixing bowl, whisk together the flour, cocoa powder, baking powder, and sea salt.
3. In a separate bowl, whisk together the applesauce, plant milk, maple syrup, and vanilla. Add the wet ingredients to the flour mixture and gently fold the two together until well incorporated.
4. Using a medium ice cream scoop or a ⅓-cup measure, scoop the batter onto a nonstick baking sheet or a regular baking sheet lined with parchment paper, making 18 cookies about 2 inches apart.
5. Bake the cookies until a toothpick inserted into the center of each cookie comes out clean, 12 to 14 minutes. Let the cookies cool to room temperature.
6. Turn the cookies flat side up and spread some of the breakfast spread over half of the cookies. Top with the remaining cookies to make sandwiches.

 **RECIPE TIP**

Desserts made without added fat burn more easily and can be very dry if over-baked. Set your timer and check the cookies before the last 5 minutes of baking. Most ovens vary by 25 degrees or more in temperature, so you can't always depend on time to check for doneness with baked goods.

RECIPE TIP

If you try to fill the cookies with the spread before the cookies have cooled completely, the spread will melt and ooze out of the cookie. Once again, patience will be rewarded!

BLONDIES

If you want to avoid giving your kids a lot of chocolate, try making these bars for them. They are full of peanut butter flavor, with just a hint of chocolate.

Makes 9 bars

1 (15-ounce) can white beans, rinsed and drained, or 1½ cups cooked white beans (see Tip)

1½ cups Date Puree (page 241)

½ cup creamy peanut butter

1 teaspoon pure vanilla extract

2 tablespoons arrowroot powder

½ cup whole wheat pastry flour or barley flour

½ teaspoon double-acting baking powder

¼ teaspoon sea salt

¾ cup vegan chocolate chips (optional)

1. Preheat the oven to 350°F.
2. Combine the beans, date puree, peanut butter, vanilla, and arrowroot powder in a food processor and puree until smooth and creamy. Transfer the bean mixture to a mixing bowl.
3. In a small bowl, whisk together the flour, baking powder, and sea salt. Add the flour mixture to the bowl with the bean mixture, along with the chocolate chips, and fold the ingredients together.
4. Spoon the batter into a nonstick 8-inch square baking pan, and gently press the batter into the pan. Bake until a toothpick inserted into the center comes out clean, 35 to 40 minutes. Let stand for 20 minutes before cutting into 9 squares.

🍽 RECIPE TIP

Any white beans will work in this recipe—Great Northern, cannellini, or navy—so use whatever you have on hand.

APPLE BUTTER PIZZA

Keep the ingredients on hand for this delicious treat and let the kids make it for themselves when they want something special for dessert.

Makes 1 (12-inch) pizza

4 Granny Smith or other tart, firm apples, peeled, cored, and thinly sliced

½ cup pure maple syrup

1 (12-ounce) jar sugar-free apple butter (about 1½ cups)

4 tablespoons creamy peanut butter

½ recipe Whole Wheat Pizza Crust (page 209), unbaked

1 recipe Vanilla-Almond Dessert Sauce (page 242)

Ground cinnamon

1. Preheat the oven to 375°F.
2. Combine the apples and maple syrup in a saucepan and cook over medium heat until the apples are tender but not mushy, 8 to 10 minutes.
3. In a small bowl, whisk together the apple butter and peanut butter.
4. Place the pizza crust on a baking sheet and shape into a 12-inch round. Spread the apple butter mixture over the pizza crust and spoon the cooked apples over it. Drizzle the dessert sauce over the apples and sprinkle with a little cinnamon.
5. Bake until the crust starts to brown on the edges, 12 to 14 minutes. Let cool for 10 minutes before serving.

ACKNOWLEDGMENTS

Many people contributed their time to making this book happen.

In addition to the very talented staff at Benbella, who make everything look beautiful, my staff here at Wellness Forum Health puts up with me and my persistent recipe testing, editing, and artistic temperament—thank you Pam Popper, Kelly Sherman, Pam Frost, Laura Payne, Garrett Colburn, Cindy Bebe, Rita the intern, Whitnie Carter, Beth Perera, and Chris Dorka.

Thanks, too, to my cooking class students, who let me experiment on them in class, and most importantly to my family, who taught me to love good food, and to all the families who were willing to step up to the plate and tell their stories.

Finally, thanks to the Campbell family, who let me be a part of their world. You are truly an amazing family.

RECIPE INDEX

B

M

Mac and Cheese, 224
- in Chili Mac and Cheese Casserole, 227

Macaroni
- in Chili Mac and Cheese Casserole, 227
- in Johnny Marzetti, 223
- in Mac and Cheese, 224

Maple Syrup
- in Apple Butter Pizza, 266
- for Biscuits, 50
- for French Toast Casserole, 77
- in Good Gravy, 102
- in Living the Dream Brownies, 254
- in Mushroom "Bacon," 122
- in Pumpkin Bars, 260–261
- for Sweet Potato Cornbread, 85
- in Thai-Style Peanut Noodles, 192
- in Whoopie Pies, 262

Mayonnaise, 97
- in Breakfast Sandwich, 68
- in "Fried Bologna" Sandwiches, 146
- in MLT Sandwiches, 149

Meatballs
- in Mediterranean Loaf, 228
- in Mediterranean "Meatball" Subs, 158
- in Mediterranean Melts, 157

Mediterranean Loaf, 228

Mediterranean "Meatball" Subs, 158

Mediterranean Melts, 157

Medjool Dates
- in Cheesecake Pops, 250
- in Chocolate-Covered Peanut Butter-Filled Dates, 245
- in French Toast Casserole, 77

Millet, 107
- in Chorizo, 62–63
- in Spaghetti and Meatballs, 199–200
- in Spicy Breakfast Patties, 56–57
- in Tortilla Pie, 235–236

Mint
- in Thai-Style Noodles with Cashews and Pineapple, 194–195

Miso
- in Caesar Salad Dressing, 120
- in Ode to Pimento Spread Sandwiches, 142
- in Portobello Pepper Steak, 196
- in Ramen, 201–202

MLTs, 149

Mushroom "Bacon," 122
- in Cobb Salad, 133
- in MLT Sandwiches, 149

Mushrooms
- in Asparagus, Leek, and Mushroom Frittata, 66–67
- in Breakfast Casserole with Hash Brown Crust, 72–73
- in "Fried Bologna" Sandwiches, 146
- in Good Gravy, 102
- in Johnny Marzetti, 223
- in MLT Sandwiches, 149
- in Mushroom "Bacon," 122
- in Portobello Pepper Steak, 196
- in Portobello Reubens, 154–155
- in Potato Soup, 171
- in Quesadillas, 187
- in Ramen, 201–202
- in Sausage, Pepper, and Mushroom Pizza, 208–209
- in Tofu Yung, 206–207

Mustard Seeds
- in Twice-Baked Samosa Potatoes, 210–211

N

Nachos, 89

Noodles
- in Ramen, 201–202
- in Spaghetti and Meatballs, 199–200
- in Thai-Style Noodles with Cashews and Pineapple, 194–195
- in Thai-Style Peanut Noodles, 192

Nut Butters
- in Apple Butter Pizza, 266
- in Blondies, 265
- in Breakfast Spread, 53
- in Chocolate-Covered Peanut Butter-Filled Dates, 245
- in Chocolate Frosting, 47–48
- in Chocolate Sweet Potato Hummus, 246
- in Chunky Monkey Cookies, 253
- in Ode to Pimento Spread Sandwiches, 142
- in Sweet Potato Bisque, 168
- in Thai-Style Peanut Noodles, 192
- in Vanilla-Almond Dessert Sauce, 242

Nutritional Yeast
- in Asparagus, Leek, and Mushroom Frittata, 66–67

ABOUT THE AUTHOR

Del Sroufe's passion for cooking began at eight years old and never faded. In 1989 he went to work for one of Columbus's premier vegetarian restaurants, the King Avenue Coffeehouse, where he honed his craft as a baker and chef. Sroufe opened Del's Bread, a vegan bakery, before beginning vegan meal delivery service in 2001, serving eclectic plant-based cuisine to Columbus residents. During this time, he developed what became a very popular cooking class series, sharing many of the delicious recipes he had created over the years.

In 2006, Sroufe joined Wellness Forum Foods as co-owner and chef, where he continued the tradition of delivering great tasting, plant-based meals to clients in Columbus as well as throughout the continental United States. Sroufe also joined The Wellness Forum as a member, where, after a lifetime of yo-yo dieting, he has lost over 200 pounds on a low-fat, plant-based diet. He continues to teach cooking classes at local venues like Whole Foods, Community Recreation Centers, and The Wellness Forum. Sroufe is the author of *The China Study: Quick & Easy Cookbook*, as well as *Forks Over Knives—The Cookbook*, a vegan cookbook companion to the acclaimed documentary *Forks Over Knives*.

THE CHINA STUDY

The Most Comprehensive Study
of Nutrition Ever Conducted

T. COLIN CAMPBELL, PhD, AND THOMAS M. CAMPBELL II, MD

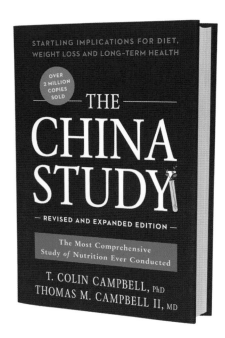

Updated and expanded edition of the bestseller that changed millions of lives

T. Colin Campbell, PhD, and Thomas M. Campbell II, MD, share their findings from the most comprehensive study ever undertaken of the relationship between diet and the risk of developing disease: You can dramatically reduce your risk just by changing to a whole food, plant-based diet.

Featuring brand-new content, this heavily expanded edition includes the latest undeniable evidence of the power of a plant-based diet, plus updated information about the changing medical system and how patients stand to benefit from a surging interest in plant-based nutrition.

For more than 40 years, T. Colin Campbell, PhD, has been at the forefront of nutrition research. Dr. Campbell is the author of the bestselling book, *The China Study*, the *New York Times* bestseller *Whole*, and *The Low-Carb Fraud* and is the Jacob Gould Schurman Professor Emeritus of Nutritional Biochemistry at Cornell University.

Thomas M. Campbell II, MD, is a board-certified family physician and the co-founder and clinical director of the University of Rochester Program for Nutrition in Medicine. In addition, Dr. Campbell is medical director of the T. Colin Campbell Center for Nutrition Studies, and author of *The China Study Solution*.

Visit THECHINASTUDY.COM to learn more!

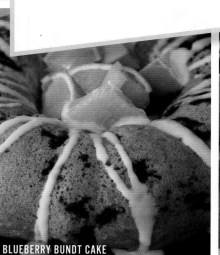